SNEAKY green uses for everyday things

How to craft eco-garments and sneaky snack
kits, create green cleaners, remake paper into
flying toys, assemble alternative energy science
projects, and construct a robot
recycle bin with everyday things

CY TYMONY

**Andrews McMeel
Publishing, LLC**

Kansas City

09 10 11 12 13 RR2 10 9 8 7 6 5 4 3 2 1

ISBN-13: 978-0-7407-7933-6
ISBN-10: 0-7407-7933-8

Library of Congress Control Number: 2008936238

www.andrewsmcmeel.com
www.sneakyuses.com

Certified Chain of Custody
60% Certified Fiber Sourcing and
40% Post-Consumer Recycled

www.sfiprogram.org

The SFI label only applies to the text stock.

ATTENTION: SCHOOLS AND BUSINESSES
Andrews McMeel books are available at quantity discounts with bulk purchase for educational, business, or sales promotional use. For information, please write to: Special Sales Department, Andrews McMeel Publishing, LLC, 1130 Walnut Street, Kansas City, Missouri 64106.

DISCLAIMER

This book is for the entertainment and edification of its readers. While reasonable care has been exercised with respect to its accuracy, the publisher and the author assume no responsibility for errors or omissions in its content. Nor do we assume liability for any damages resulting from use of the information presented here.

This book contains references to electrical safety that *must* be observed. *Do not use AC power for any projects listed.* Do not place or store magnets near such magnetically sensitive media as videotapes, audiotapes, or computer disks.

Disparities in materials and design methods and the application of the components may cause results to vary from those shown here. The publisher and the author disclaim any liability for injury that may result from the use, proper or improper, of the information contained in this book. We do not guarantee that the information contained herein is complete, safe, or accurate, nor should it be considered a substitute for your good judgment and common sense.

Nothing in this book should be construed or interpreted to infringe on the rights of other persons or to violate criminal statutes. We urge you to obey all laws and respect all rights, including property rights, of others.

Contents

PART I

SNEAKY ENERGY PROJECTS AND SIMULATIONS . . . 1

PART II

SNEAKY PRODUCT REUSE PROJECTS . . . 45

PART III
SNEAKY RECYCLING PROJECTS . . . 87

ECO-RESOURCES...**121**

ACKNOWLEDGMENTS

I'd like to thank my agents, Sheree Bykofsky and Janet Rosen, for believing in my Sneaky Uses book concept from the start.

Special thanks to Katie Anderson, my Andrews McMeel editor, for her valuable support. I'm also grateful to the following people who helped spread the word about the first five Sneaky Uses books: Ira Flatow, Gayle Anderson, Susan Casey, Mark Frauenfelder, Sandy Cohen, Katey Schwartz, Cherie Courtade, Mike Suan, John Schatzel, Melissa Gwynne, Steve Cochran, Christopher G. Selfridge, Timothy M. Blangger, Charles Bergquist, Phillip M. Torrone, Paul and Zan Dubin Scott, Dana Vinke, Cynthia Hansen, Charles Powell, Harmonie Tangonan, and Bruce Pasarow. I'm thankful for project evaluation and testing assistance provided by Sybil Smith, Isaac English, and Bill Melzer. And a special thanks to Helen Cooper, Clyde Tymony, George and Zola Wright, Ronald Mitchell, and to my mother, Cloise Shaw, for providing positive motivation, resources, and support for an early foundation in science, and a love of reading.

Introduction

Deep inside, every conservationist hates waste. They love to save energy, prevent using unnecessary product packaging and want to reuse items in new ways. Yet, most *green* books just provide a long list of energy, and product manufacturing statistics, and only fundamental recycling tips. However, when you learn how to reuse or re-adapt broken or discarded items into other useful gear, you save money, reduce air pollution, and gain a sense of contentment that comes with self-reliance.

That's what *Sneaky Green Uses for Everyday Things* does. It provides an easy way to learn: the fundamentals of energy production, alternative energy science projects, sneaky recycling techniques, and fun reuse activities.

You don't have to be MacGyver to give gadgets a second life. Anyone can learn how to be a real-life improviser in minutes using nothing but paper, cardboard, and other hodgepodge items fate has put at his or her disposal. *Sneaky Green Uses for Everyday Things* is packed with projects and activities all utilizing savvy product reuse applications. For lovers of savvy conservation and recycling activities, *Sneaky Green Uses for Everyday Things* is an amazing assortment of easy-to-understand energy fundamentals, conservation facts, and over forty innovative reuse projects.

After building a project or two, you'll be inspired to create other eco-crafts and share your sneaky green designs with your family and friends. Hopefully they will never look at "waste" the same way again and perhaps they will even become eco-trashformers themselves!

You can start your entry into sneaky green resourcefulness here.

SNEAKY GREEN USES FOR EVERYDAY THINGS

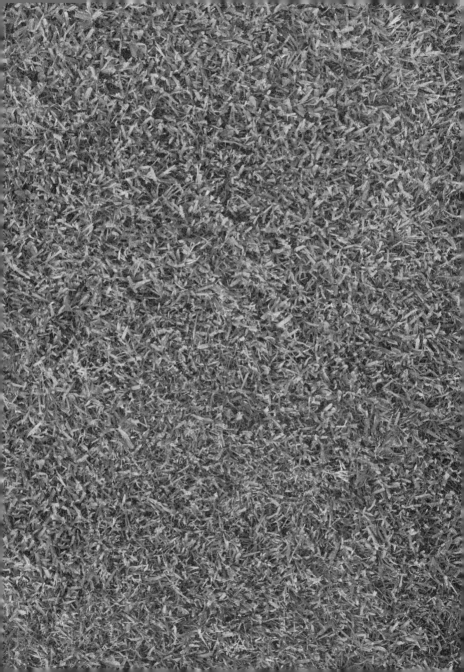

PART I

SNEAKY ENERGY PROJECTS AND SIMULATIONS

Energy affects all of our lives. We depend on it for transportation, industry, and to power our homes, as well as for hundreds of other uses you might never consider. With so many standard and emerging alternative energy sources available, it's no wonder that the average person doesn't know the fundamental methods utilized to obtain, produce, and distribute energy. This section includes background details and activities to explain energy fundamentals and help you understand them.

Do you know how oil is refined and how biofuels can substitute for gasoline and diesel fuel? Why uranium must be enriched? The difference in a standard gasoline engine and a diesel? If you're curious about how a hybrid car can utilize normally wasted energy during braking or want details about atomic energy then this section is for you. You'll learn the basic techniques used to obtain energy from coal, oil, gas, the sun, wind, and water—and from the atom.

Whether you want to know energy theory or have a guide to making unique energy-related science simulations, this section's projects expand anyone's knowledge in a fun and interesting way to help you make more informed choices.

ENERGY FUNDAMENTALS

Energy is what makes things change or move. It is found in many forms, including heat, chemical, light, electrical, and mechanical energy.

Kinetic energy is the energy in moving things. Energy that can be stored for later use is called *potential energy.* Gases, solids, and chemicals can all store potential energy that may be released later in a variety of ways.

For instance, when certain substances, such as coal, are burned, the process releases energy in the form of heat. In a coal-fired electrical power plant, the heat that the released energy produces is used to boil water into steam, which in turn propels turbine blades to power an electrical generator. See **Figure 1**.

Food, oil, and batteries have potential energy stored within their chemicals. Springs and rubber bands do, as well. They can be wound up to store *strain energy* for later use.

Energy can be converted from one form or another for practical use. Common energy conversions take place all the time, all around you. For example:

- The sun provides energy for plants to make food. This food is stored as *chemical energy.* When animals eat plants, they convert the chemical energy into motion and heat.
- Chemical energy is stored in consumer batteries, where it is converted into electricity. The electricity is changed into heat, light, motion, or sound, depending on whether the batteries are in a flashlight, toy, radio, or other device.

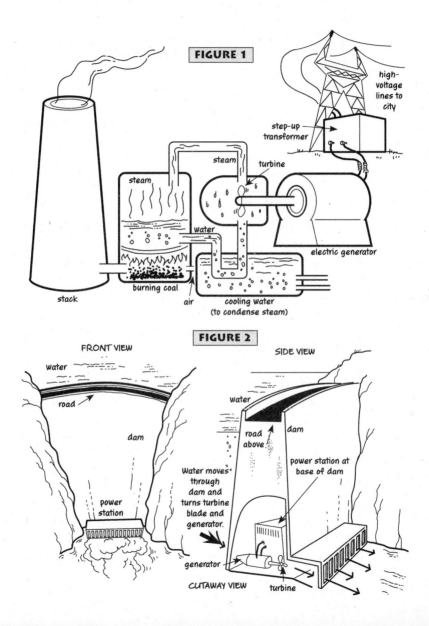

FIGURE 1

high-voltage lines to city

step-up transformer

steam

turbine

steam

water

electric generator

steam

burning coal

air

cooling water (to condense steam)

stack

FIGURE 2

FRONT VIEW

water

road

dam

power station

SIDE VIEW

water

road above

dam

power station at base of dam

Water moves through dam and turns turbine blade and generator.

generator

CUTAWAY VIEW

turbine

⚜ Hydroelectric power plants use water at a high elevation to fall on turbine blades, which turn electrical generators. As shown in **Figure 2**, water, blocked by a dam, flows through a penstock channel where it eventually reaches a turbine. The rushing water spins the turbine blades and provides mechanical energy to an electrical generator.

⚜ Wood, oil, and coal store energy from the sun as chemical energy. In the case of gas, oil, and coal, they are burned to release chemical energy in the form of heat. Geothermal power plants use underground pockets of steam to power turbines.

Electrical power stations have large water, gas, or steam turbines that turn electrical generators. An electrical generator diagram is shown in **Figure 3**. To reduce energy loss while traveling over long-distance power lines, step-up transformers increase the voltage level from about 15,000 to 20,000 volts, to several hundred thousand volts. Electric power substations, located near cities, use distribution transformers to step down the voltage to about 7,200 volts. Line transformers, near homes and businesses, step down the voltage level to 240 volts.

Wires leading from line transformers can be tapped to produce 120 volts, for most needs, or 240 volts for heavy-duty appliances such as washers and dryers. See **Figure 4**.

The next project illustrates an easy-to-make multistage example of energy storage and conversion.

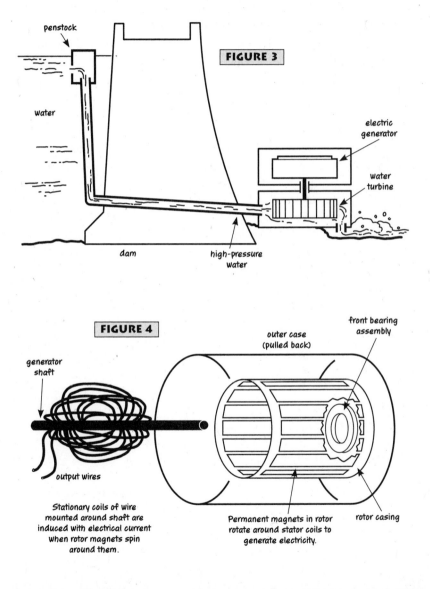

FIGURE 3

penstock

water

electric generator

water turbine

dam

high-pressure water

FIGURE 4

generator shaft

outer case (pulled back)

front bearing assembly

output wires

Stationary coils of wire mounted around shaft are induced with electrical current when rotor magnets spin around them.

Permanent magnets in rotor rotate around stator coils to generate electricity.

rotor casing

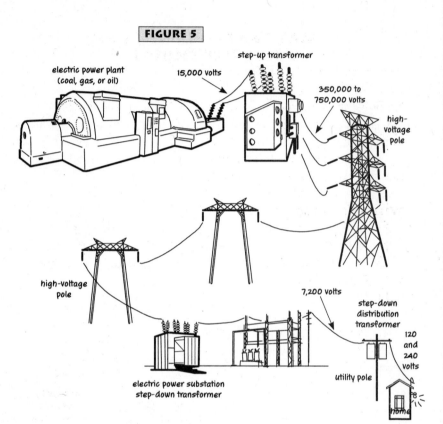

FIGURE 5

electric power plant
(coal, gas, or oil)

15,000 volts

step-up transformer

350,000 to
750,000 volts

high-
voltage
pole

high-voltage
pole

7,200 volts

step-down
distribution
transformer

120
and
240
volts

utility pole

electric power substation
step-down transformer

home

MAKE BATTERIES FROM EVERYDAY THINGS

No one can dispute the usefulness of electricity. But what do you do if you're in a remote area without AC power or batteries? Make sneaky batteries, of course!

In this project, you'll learn how to use fruits, vegetable juices, paper clips, and coins to generate electricity.

WHAT'S NEEDED

- Lemon or other fruit
- Nail
- Heavy copper wire
- Paper clip or twist-tie
- Water
- Salt
- Paper towel
- Pennies and nickels
- Plate

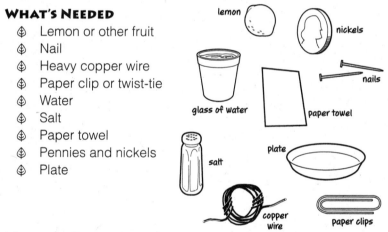

WHAT TO DO
THE FRUIT BATTERY

Insert a nail or paper clip into a lemon. Then stick a piece of heavy copper wire into the lemon. Make sure that the wire is close to, but does not touch, the nail (see **Figure 1**). The nail has become the battery's negative electrode and the copper wire is the positive electrode. The lemon juice, which is acidic, acts as the electrolyte. You can use other item pairs besides a paper clip

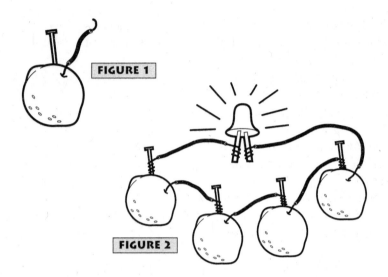

and copper wire, as long as they are made of different metals. The lemon battery will supply about one-fourth to one-third of a volt of electricity. To use a sneaky battery as the battery to power a small electrical device, like an LED light, you must connect a few of them in a series, as shown in **Figure 2**. Note: If the LED does not light, reverse the connections on its leads.

THE COIN BATTERY

With the fruit battery, you stuck the metal into the fruit. You can also make a battery by placing a chemical solution between two coins.

Dissolve 2 tablespoons of salt in a glass of water. This is the electrolyte you will place between two dissimilar metal coins.

Now moisten a piece of paper towel or tissue in the salt water. Put a nickel on a plate and put a small piece of the wet absorbent paper on the nickel. Then place a penny on top of the paper. Next place another moistened piece of paper towel and then another nickel on top of the penny and continue the series until you have a stack.

In order for the homemade battery to do useful work, you must make a series of stacked coins and paper.

Be sure the paper separators do not touch one another.

The more pairs of coins you add, the higher the voltage output will be. One coin pair should produce about one-third of a volt. With six pairs stacked up, you should be able to power a small flashlight bulb, LED, or other device when the regular batteries have failed. See **Figure 3**. Power will last up to two hours.

Once you know how to make sneaky batteries, you'll never again be totally out of power sources.

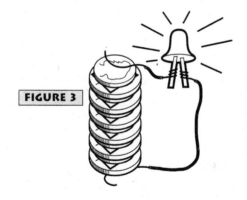

FIGURE 3

SNEAKY ELECTRICAL GENERATOR

New energy sources are being found and refined every day, and you can demonstrate how industry, smaller businesses, and individuals take advantage of various forms of alternate energy sources. This project illustrates three methods that harness the power of wind, water, and steam to produce electricity.

When a wire moves near a magnet, an electrical current is induced. Using this knowledge, you can create a Sneaky Electrical Generator with a toy motor.

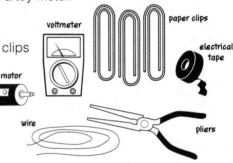

WHAT'S NEEDED

- ⊕ Three large paper clips
- ⊕ Electrical tape
- ⊕ Toy car motor
- ⊕ Pliers
- ⊕ Voltmeter
- ⊕ Wire (optional)

WHAT TO DO

First, bend the three paper clips into the shapes shown in **Figure 1**. Paper clip one will act as a hand crank. The other two paper clips will act as propeller blades.

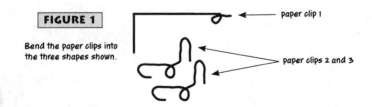

FIGURE 1

Bend the paper clips into the three shapes shown.

paper clip 1

paper clips 2 and 3

Next, wrap electrical tape around the shaft of the toy car motor. See **Figure 2**.

If the motor does not have wires on its two terminals, tape two 4-inch lengths of wire to them with tape.

Then, attach the first paper clip to the motor shaft and press it tight with pliers. Place the voltmeter on its lowest direct current (DC) setting and wrap the motor wires around its probes. Cranking the motor should cause the voltmeter to indicate a current has been generated, as shown in **Figure 3**.

Next, remove the first paper clip and press the other two paper clips onto the motor shaft as shown in **Figure 4**. Reshape the first paper clip to resemble the other two and press it onto the motor shaft also. See **Figure 5**.

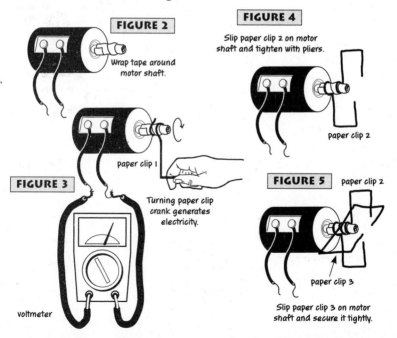

FIGURE 2

Wrap tape around motor shaft.

FIGURE 4

Slip paper clip 2 on motor shaft and tighten with pliers.

paper clip 2

paper clip 1

FIGURE 3

Turning paper clip crank generates electricity.

voltmeter

FIGURE 5

paper clip 2

paper clip 3

Slip paper clip 3 on motor shaft and secure it tightly.

Apply tape to all three paper clips to form propeller blades, as shown in **Figure 6**.

If you blow on the propeller or use a small hair dryer on it, the blades will turn and you will be harnessing wind power to generate electricity.

You can carefully hold the motor blades near a teakettle spout to harness steam power or place the propeller under a faucet's stream of running water to harness hydro power as shown in **Figure 7**.

Note: If you have a personal battery-powered fan, you can connect it to the voltmeter and spin its blades with your fingers to attain the same effect. See **Figure 8**.

Figure 9 illustrates the internal parts of a wind turbine. Multiple wind turbines, called a wind farm, are shown in **Figure 10**.

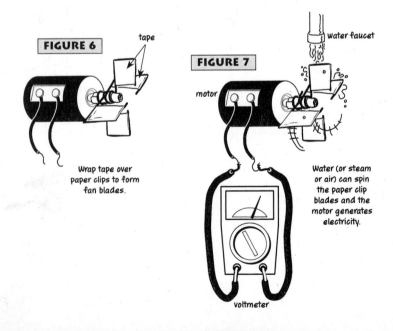

FIGURE 6

tape

Wrap tape over paper clips to form fan blades.

FIGURE 7

water faucet

motor

Water (or steam or air) can spin the paper clip blades and the motor generates electricity.

voltmeter

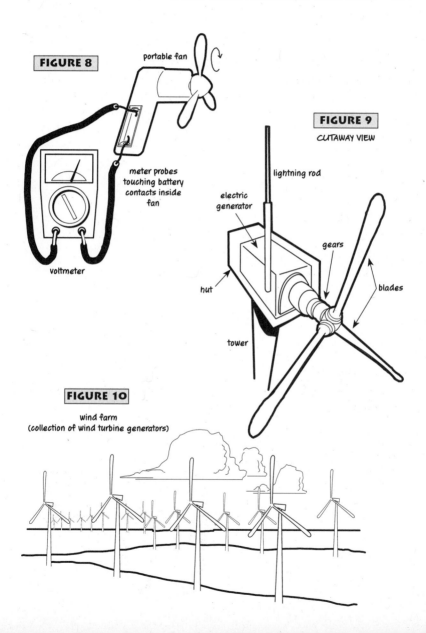

FIGURE 8

portable fan

meter probes
touching battery
contacts inside
fan

voltmeter

FIGURE 9

CUTAWAY VIEW

lightning rod

electric
generator

gears

blades

hut

tower

FIGURE 10

wind farm
(collection of wind turbine generators)

HAND-POWERED FAN

As you may know, hot air rises. Rising heat can be made to move objects, and you can demonstrate this fact with a novel "hand-powered" motor. In this demonstrational science project, your hands will actually provide the heat to demonstrate how moving air currents can move an object in a rotary motion.

All it takes is an ordinary piece of paper, scissors, a needle, a cardboard box, and your hands.

WHAT'S NEEDED

- ✤ Paper
- ✤ Scissors
- ✤ Sewing needle
- ✤ Small cardboard box

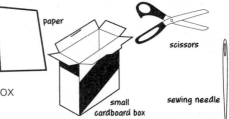

paper

scissors

small cardboard box

sewing needle

WHAT TO DO

Cut a piece of paper into a 2-inch square. Fold it in half diagonally; then unfold it and fold it in half on the other diagonal, as shown in **Figure 1**. This should create a cross-fold with a center point.

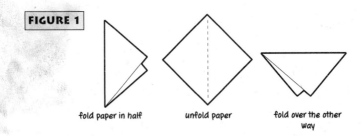

FIGURE 1

fold paper in half   unfold paper   fold over the other way

You can use a paper-clip box or similar small box as a mount for the needle. Hold the needle on its side with your fingers and carefully twist it into the top of the box (or use a thimble) until it punctures a hole in the top. Place the piece of paper on top of the needle so its center point allows the paper to turn freely. See **Figure 2**.

To make the sneaky "motor" turn, rub your hands together back and forth about twenty times to generate heat and place them near the sides of the paper. After a few seconds, the paper will begin to spin (**Figure 3**).

The paper spins because the heat on your hands causes a temperature increase in the air around the paper. As the heated air rises and cooler air takes its place, the air movement pushes the paper sides, causing it to rotate like a motor.

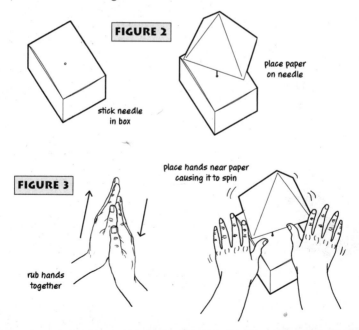

FIGURE 2

stick needle
in box

place paper
on needle

FIGURE 3

rub hands
together

place hands near paper
causing it to spin

SNEAKY HYBRID CAR DEMONSTRATION

Hybrid cars utilize two different methods of power—usually a gas combustion engine and an electrical motor—to power the vehicle. Depending on the design, a hybrid car can use one type of power for initial movement at low speeds and then another form of propulsion at higher speed, to optimize gas savings. Some hybrid models use both types of power simultaneously to complement each other.

For instance, a Toyota Prius hybrid initially uses an electric motor for low speeds, usually under 10 miles per hour, and switches to its gasoline engine for high-speed operation.

During braking, standard vehicles use mechanical pressure against brake drums or disks to slow the vehicle. Energy is lost as heat during this process. The Prius has another power-saving technology: a second, smaller motor/generator uses energy normally lost to heat during braking, to recharge its battery or act as a motor itself to add power to the engine's output. See **Figure 1**.

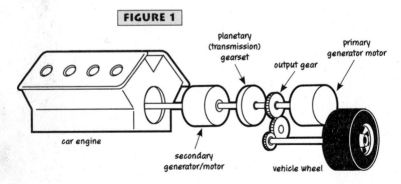

FIGURE 1

planetary (transmission) gearset

primary generator motor

output gear

car engine

secondary generator/motor

vehicle wheel

This project will show how to make a hybrid car that stores energy for use when the primary source is not active.

WHAT'S NEEDED

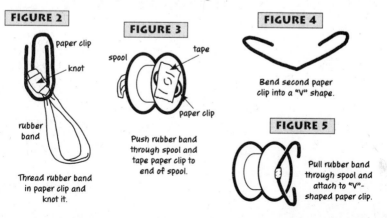

- Rubber band
- Two paper clips
- Wire or thread spool
- Transparent tape
- 1 large paper clip
- Toy wire- or radio-controlled car

paper clips

tape

toy car

rubber band

wire spool

WHAT TO DO

First, thread the rubber band into the opening of a regular paper clip and back through the hole on the other end of the rubber band. Pull tightly until a knot is formed, as shown in **Figure 2**. Push the rubber band through the spool and use tape to secure the paper clip to the outside. See **Figure 3**.

Bend another regular paper clip into a **V** shape, as shown in **Figure 4**. Slip the loose end of the rubber band onto the middle of the **V**-shaped paper clip. See **Figure 5**.

FIGURE 2

paper clip

knot

rubber band

Thread rubber band in paper clip and knot it.

FIGURE 3

spool

tape

paper clip

Push rubber band through spool and tape paper clip to end of spool.

FIGURE 4

Bend second paper clip into a "V" shape.

FIGURE 5

Pull rubber band through spool and attach to "V"-shaped paper clip.

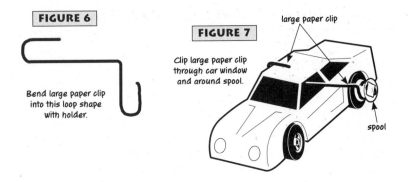

FIGURE 6

Bend large paper clip
into this loop shape
with holder.

FIGURE 7

large paper clip

Clip large paper clip
through car window
and around spool.

spool

Next, bend the large paper clip so that one side has a round hook to hold the spool (see **Figure 6**) and the other end will fit through the toy car window. **Figure 7** shows how to mount the spool onto the large paper clip and secure it to the car.

Next, bend the large paper clip so the spool will touch the floor surface and spin when the car moves on the floor. Using the remote control, run the toy car in circles on the floor at least five times around the room. Carefully lift the car while holding the spool. Pull the spool off the large paper clip and set it on the floor. It will spin on its own because the rubber band was wound by the toy car's movement.

SOLAR POWER GENERATOR

Solar cells convert light from the sun into electricity. A photovoltaic (PV) cell is a semiconductor that needs a little energy to allow electron flow between its N- and P-type layers. Solar cells have a protective cover, an antireflective coating, and electrical contacts that collect photons, particles of solar energy, and transfer them into electric current. See **Figure 1**.

Solar cells can be removed from small toys and calculators or purchased separately from electronic parts supply houses and hobby stores.

You can demonstrate how solar power can be used to power devices by connecting a solar cell to a miniature radio-controlled car.

WHAT'S NEEDED

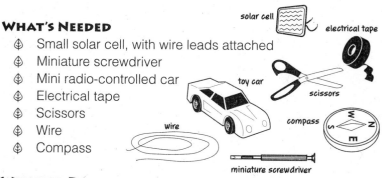

solar cell

electrical tape

toy car

scissors

compass

wire

miniature screwdriver

- Small solar cell, with wire leads attached
- Miniature screwdriver
- Mini radio-controlled car
- Electrical tape
- Scissors
- Wire
- Compass

WHAT TO DO

First, obtain a small solar cell with wire leads already attached (so you do not have to solder).

Next, carefully remove the body from the mini radio-controlled car. Most models allow you to pry off the body from the chassis with a miniature flat-bladed screwdriver. The motor can usually be

FIGURE 1

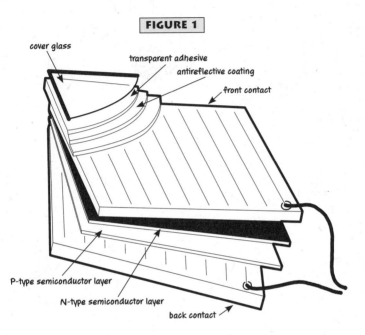

cover glass

transparent adhesive

antireflective coating

front contact

P-type semiconductor layer

N-type semiconductor layer

back contact

lifted out of the chassis once the motor cover (if found) is pried open as shown in **Figure 2**.

Connect the solar cell wires to the terminals of the motor with tape, as shown in **Figure 3**. If you only see one terminal or wire, the motor casing is its negative (–) terminal. Place the solar cell and motor under a bright light or in the sun and it should start to spin.

The car should move on its own when exposed to sunlight and, possibly, a bright room lamp. See **Figure 4**.

Wire that is connected to the solar cell can move a compass needle when it's wrapped around a compass. See **Figure 5**.

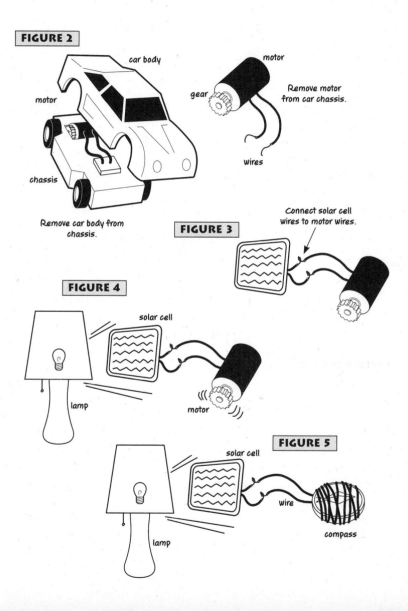

FIGURE 2

car body

motor

chassis

motor

gear

wires

Remove motor from car chassis.

Remove car body from chassis.

FIGURE 3

Connect solar cell wires to motor wires.

FIGURE 4

solar cell

lamp

motor

FIGURE 5

solar cell

lamp

wire

compass

SNEAKY HYDROGEN POWER DEMONSTRATION

Hydrogen is an energy carrier, not an energy source. In the future, hydrogen fuel cells will be virtually emission-free forms of energy storage devices.

Fuel cells use a chemical reaction to produce electricity by combining hydrogen and oxygen. A diagram of a polymer electrolyte membrane (PEM) fuel cell is shown in **Figure 1**. Hydrogen enters the fuel cell's anode, where its electrons and protons are separated. The protons pass through the PEM while the electrons are forced to take an external route, which makes electricity. Oxygen is fed into the cathode side and combines with the protons and electrons to form water. The cycle repeats and produces an electrical current. See **Figure 2**. This process is called *electrolysis*.

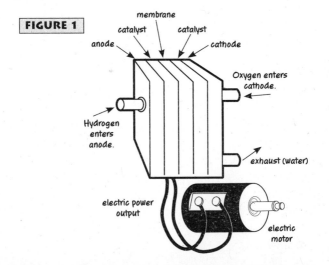

FIGURE 2

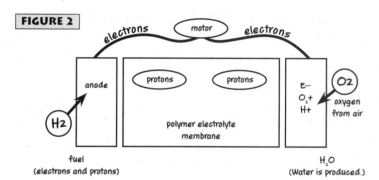

fuel
(electrons and protons)

H_2O
(Water is produced.)

You can demonstrate this process by separating water (H_2O, composed of hydrogen and oxygen) into its two elements with electricity.

WHAT'S NEEDED

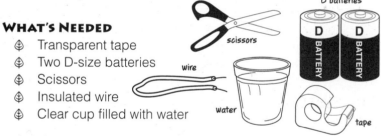

- ⚡ Transparent tape
- ⚡ Two D-size batteries
- ⚡ Scissors
- ⚡ Insulated wire
- ⚡ Clear cup filled with water

WHAT TO DO

Tape the two D-size batteries together with one positive end connected to the negative end of the other. See **Figure 3**.

Cut two pieces of insulated wire and strip the insulation from both ends of them. Tape the wires to the ends of the battery terminals, as shown in **Figure 4**.

Next, place both of the free wire ends in the cup of water. See **Figure 5**. You should soon see bubbles appear on the ends of the wire lead. One of them will have about twice as many bubbles. This is hydrogen gas separating from the oxygen, as shown in **Figure 6**.

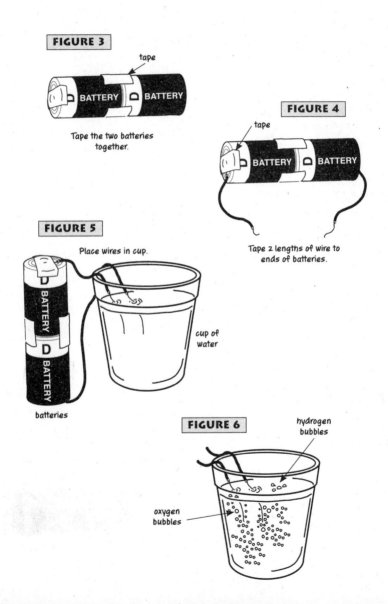

FIGURE 3

tape

BATTERY BATTERY

Tape the two batteries
together.

FIGURE 4

tape

BATTERY BATTERY

Tape 2 lengths of wire to
ends of batteries.

FIGURE 5

Place wires in cup.

BATTERY

BATTERY

cup of
water

batteries

FIGURE 6

hydrogen
bubbles

oxygen
bubbles

SNEAKY MOTOR

When electrical current passes through a wire it produces a magnetic field that will attract some metals and other magnets. You can make a simple electromagnet with a battery, wire, and a nail or bolt.

When you press the wire ends against the battery, the current flow induces a magnetic field in the coil of wire. The nail amplifies the effect and you can attract small metallic objects or a magnet. Magnets have a north and south pole, and so does your electromagnet. If you turn the magnet over, it will be either attracted to or repelled by the nail.

Using this knowledge, you can create a Sneaky Motor using the same parts in a different way.

WHAT'S NEEDED

- Transparent tape
- Three D-size batteries, one of which is to be used as a mold
- Cardboard
- Two paper clips
- Ten feet of insulated 14-gauge magnet wire
- Strong disk-shaped or square magnet
- Pliers

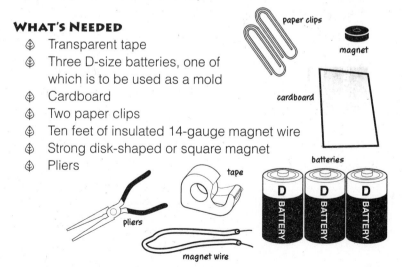

What to Do

For this Sneaky Motor, you must use magnet wire found at electronic parts or hardware stores. Although it appears to be regular copper wire, it has copper-colored insulation that can be scraped off.

Tape two D-size batteries next to each other on to the cardboard as shown in **Figure 1**. Bend the two paper clips, as shown in **Figure 2**, and tape them to the ends of the batteries, perpendicular to the terminal ends so that they extend out in front of the batteries.

Next, wrap the wire around one D-size battery twelve times and wrap the ends to form a loop (making sure to leave a wire end free on each side of the coil), as shown in **Figures 3** and **4**. Then, very carefully use the rough inner surface of the pliers to scrape just one side of each end of the wires as shown in **Figure 5**. Do not scrape off the entire insulation, just one side (180 degrees).

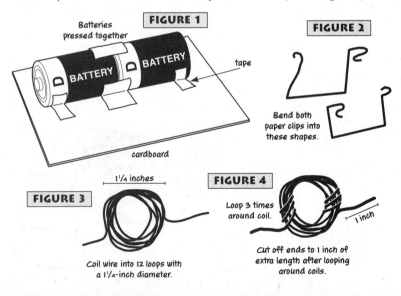

FIGURE 1

Batteries pressed together

BATTERY BATTERY

tape

cardboard

FIGURE 2

Bend both paper clips into these shapes.

FIGURE 3

1¼ inches

Coil wire into 12 loops with a 1¼-inch diameter.

FIGURE 4

Loop 3 times around coil.

1 inch

Cut off ends to 1 inch of extra length after looping around coils.

Then, place the wire coil on the paper clip hooks and position the magnet below the wire coil. Finally, spin the coil, which should continue spinning on its own. If it does not, turn the coil around or reposition the magnet until it spins freely. See **Figure 6**.

When the coil is at rest, the insulation on the ends prevents battery power from flowing through it. When you spin the coil, the bare wire touches the paper clips and the battery current flows through the wire coil, inducing a magnetic field in it. This field repels the magnet and the coil turns. When the insulated side of the coil touches the paper clips, the current stops but the momentum keeps it going until the bare wire makes contact again.

You may wonder why you bare only one side of the coil ends. If the coil wire ends were completely bare, the coil would start to spin but then immediately stop because the coil's other side, or magnetic pole, would then attract the magnet. In addition, this constant current flow would cause the battery to heat and to rapidly lose power.

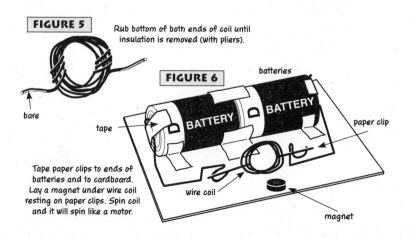

FIGURE 5

Rub bottom of both ends of coil until insulation is removed (with pliers).

bare

FIGURE 6

batteries

BATTERY   BATTERY

tape

paper clip

Tape paper clips to ends of batteries and to cardboard. Lay a magnet under wire coil resting on paper clips. Spin coil and it will spin like a motor.

wire coil

magnet

SNEAKY OIL REFINERY DEMONSTRATION

Over 60 percent of the world's energy is derived from oil and natural gas. Much as time and pressure can turn coal into diamonds, organic remains from plants and animals were converted to oil deposits by millions of years of heat and pressure.

Basically, when oil is discovered, it is brought to the surface, gas and water are removed, and what remains is then pumped through pipelines to a refinery. An oil rig at sea and an oil refinery are shown in **Figures 1** and **2**. This project will illustrate how an oil refinery converts crude oil into useful products, including gasoline.

In a refinery, crude oil is pumped into a large furnace and boiled into a gas. It is then pumped into a distillation tower to condense back into different liquid substances at various temperatures. You've witnessed evidence of condensation on a cold glass of liquid, or on grass in the early morning in the form of dew droplets. The water in the air turns into a liquid when it comes in contact with a cooler surface.

A refinery's distillation tower uses the same principle to gather different types of oil products as the heated oil condenses. **Figure 3** shows the distillation tower, which has multiple levels of saucer-shaped cool surfaces against which the oil will form condensation (liquid). This condensation drips into trays and flows to gathering tanks. The higher tanks gather oil that is cooler than what is produced in the lower ones. By this process, the key ingredients for various petroleum products, including bitumen, diesel, gasoline, kerosene, and plastics, are obtained.

You can demonstrate how a refinery works, using common items found in every kitchen.

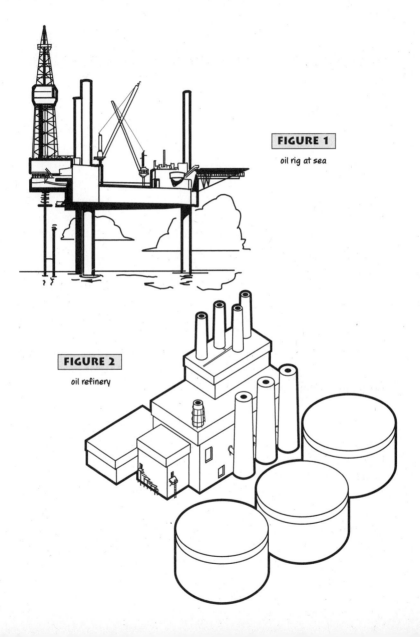

FIGURE 1

oil rig at sea

FIGURE 2

oil refinery

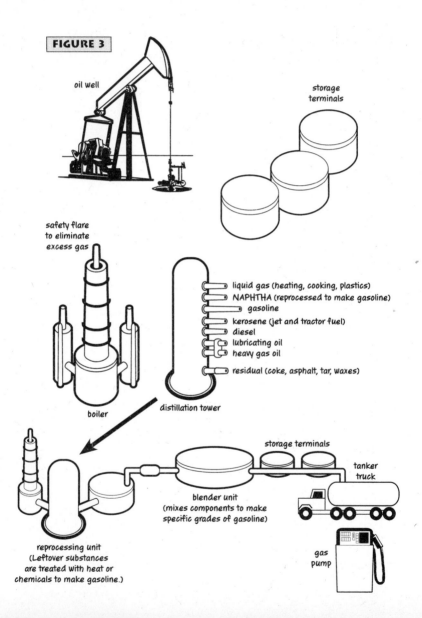

FIGURE 3

oil well

storage terminals

safety flare to eliminate excess gas

liquid gas (heating, cooking, plastics)
NAPHTHA (reprocessed to make gasoline)
gasoline
kerosene (jet and tractor fuel)
diesel
lubricating oil
heavy gas oil
residual (coke, asphalt, tar, waxes)

boiler

distillation tower

storage terminals

tanker truck

blender unit
(mixes components to make
specific grades of gasoline)

reprocessing unit
(Leftover substances
are treated with heat or
chemicals to make gasoline.)

gas pump

WHAT'S NEEDED

- Teakettle filled with water
- Bowl
- Metal pan
- Ice cubes
- Oven mitt

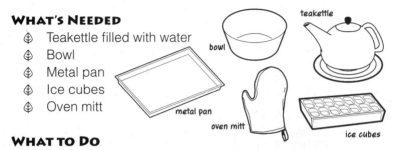

WHAT TO DO

Bring water to a boil in the teakettle. Place a bowl near the stove a few inches away from the kettle, as shown in **Figure 1**.

Next, fill the metal pan with ice cubes. See **Figure 2**. With an oven mitt, hold the pan over the bowl, near the kettle's spout, as shown in **Figure 3**.

When the steam gathers on the pan's bottom surface, which is cooled by the ice cubes, it condenses (turns into a liquid), and drips into the bowl.

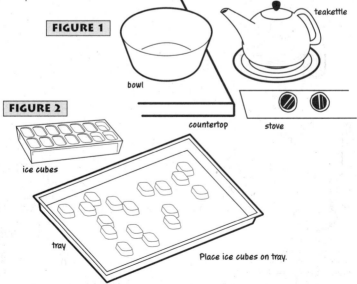

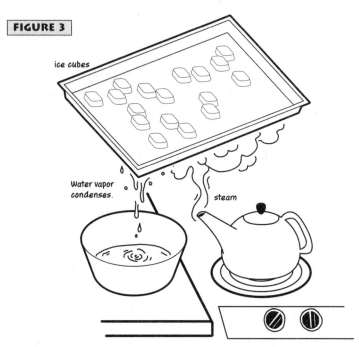

| FIGURE 3 |

ice cubes

Water vapor condenses.

steam

Biofuels

Biofuels are liquid fuels derived from crops. They include methanol (wood alcohol), ethanol (grain alcohol), and biodiesel.

Biodiesel

Rudolf Diesel made diesel engines in 1895 that could run on peanut oil. Diesel engines differ from gasoline engines because of their higher compression ratio.

Currently, in the United States, diesel cars account for less than 4 percent of the market while in Europe over 50 percent of passenger vehicles are diesel powered. A diesel engine produces higher torque at lower RPMs (rotations per minute) and gets better gas mileage, compared with its gasoline counterpart.

Standard gasoline engines use a spark plug to ignite the air-fuel mixture as shown in **Figure 1**.

In a diesel engine, the pistons compress the air-fuel mixture in the cylinder so much that the extreme heat ignites it without requiring a spark plug. See **Figure 2**.

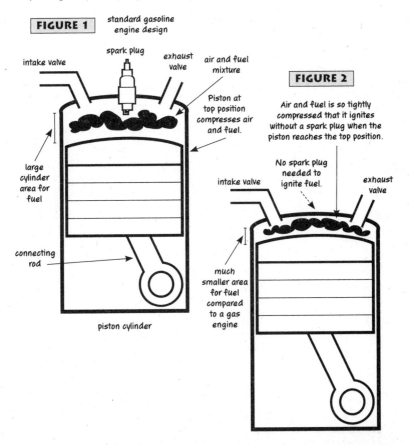

FIGURE 1   standard gasoline engine design

intake valve

spark plug

exhaust valve

air and fuel mixture

Piston at top position compresses air and fuel.

large cylinder area for fuel

connecting rod

piston cylinder

FIGURE 2

Air and fuel is so tightly compressed that it ignites without a spark plug when the piston reaches the top position.

No spark plug needed to ignite fuel.

intake valve

exhaust valve

much smaller area for fuel compared to a gas engine

All diesel engines can use biodiesel fuel if it is heated and filtered properly. Biodiesel can be made, via a chemical process, from recycled cooking oil, animal fats, soy, corn, sunflower seeds, canola, peanuts, mustard seeds, or cottonseeds. Solar energy, combined with water and carbon dioxide, provides the stored energy captured by feedstock.

Even ordinary vegetable oil or filtered cooking oil from restaurants can power biodiesel-ready vehicles.

Since the crops use carbon dioxide from the atmosphere in their energy absorption process, they are virtually a carbon-neutral source of fuel. When the vehicle's exhaust emits carbon dioxide, it's absorbed by crops and the biodiesel carbon cycle continues, as shown in **Figure 3**.

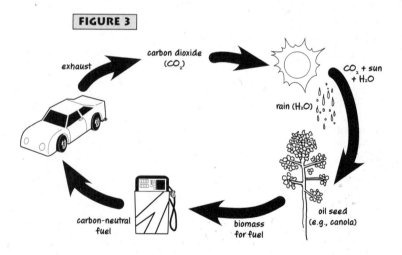

FIGURE 3

exhaust

carbon dioxide (CO_2)

CO_2 + sun + H_2O

rain (H_2O)

oil seed (e.g., canola)

biomass for fuel

carbon-neutral fuel

BIODIESEL CARBON CYCLE

SNEAKY ETHANOL DEMONSTRATION

Ethanol has been used to power vehicles since the early twentieth century—Henry Ford had ethanol-fueled Model T vehicles. Ethanol (specifically, E85—a mixture of 85 percent ethanol and 15 percent gasoline) vehicles have been available for consumers since 1992.

Ethanol can also be produced from biomass feedstocks, including corn stalks, grasses, paper, wood wastes (e.g., wood chips and sawdust), and green wastes (e.g., vegetable and fruit wastes, leaves, and grass clippings).

Figure 1 illustrates the basic ethanol production process. Corn is crushed and mixed with water. It is heated and mixed with enzymes to convert its starch into sugar. Then, it is fermented with yeast to make alcohol. To boost the alcohol content, the mixture is boiled and then dehydrated.

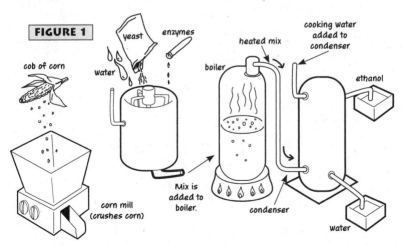

FIGURE 1

cob of corn

corn mill
(crushes corn)

water

yeast   enzymes

Mix is
added to
boiler.

boiler

heated mix

cooking water
added to
condenser

condenser

ethanol

water

Ethanol emits cleaner emissions (carbon dioxide or CO_2, carbon monoxide, and particulate emissions) compared with gasoline and diesel fuel.

This project will enable you to demonstrate how sugar breaks down into ethyl alcohol, ethanol, and carbon dioxide.

WHAT'S NEEDED

- Two cups of water
- 5 cubes of dry yeast
- Two-liter bottle
- ¼ cup of corn syrup
- Balloon

water *2-liter bottle* *corn syrup* *dry yeast* *balloon*

WHAT TO DO

First, pour the 2 cups of water and 5 cubes of yeast into the bottle and mix them by shaking the bottle for one minute. See **Figure 2**.

Then, pour the ¼ cup of corn syrup in the bottle and shake it for a minute. Wrap the lip of the balloon over the mouth of the bottle, as shown in **Figure 3**. Let the bottle sit, and monitor the liquid and the balloon every two hours.

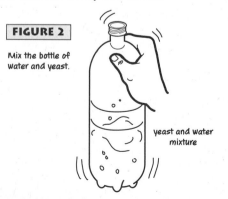

FIGURE 2

Mix the bottle of water and yeast.

yeast and water mixture

You will first see some bubbles appear on the surface of the mixture, and eventually the balloon will inflate. Fermentation is taking place. This is the process by which the yeast breaks down the sugar in the corn syrup into ethyl alcohol (ethanol) and carbon dioxide (which rises and inflates the balloon). See **Figure 4**.

You can also perform this demonstration by substituting a cola drink or table sugar for the corn syrup. Try testing all three mixtures with three separate bottles and note the amount of time for bubbles to form and the rate of inflation of the balloon.

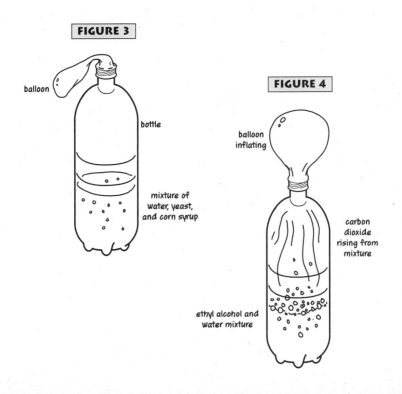

FIGURE 3

balloon

bottle

mixture of water, yeast, and corn syrup

FIGURE 4

balloon inflating

carbon dioxide rising from mixture

ethyl alcohol and water mixture

NUCLEAR ENERGY SIMULATION

This project will illustrate the multiple stages of nuclear energy production and power distribution, using everyday items. It's a perfect simulation for a school science project. First, let's review how nuclear energy is produced and converted into a form that can be used by consumers.

Similar to other power plants, nuclear power plants produce heat energy to boil water into steam that runs a turbine, which in turn powers an electrical generator. The main difference is that the heat is generated from a nuclear reaction (fission) in a lead-lined reactor, rather than without fission from burning coal.

Radioactive material, such as uranium, is mined and enriched. Once the U-235 materials are collected, they are stored as pellets inside aluminum rods. When placed near other rods, stray neutrons will start a nuclear fusion chain reaction, producing tremendous heat energy. To control the nuclear fission process, control rods are placed near them.

Control rods have pellets of cadmium or boron inside them, which absorb neutrons to halt the fission reaction. The control rods are placed between the U-235 rods in a matrix pattern (U-235 rod, control rod, U-235 rod, and so on), as shown in **Figure 1**.

When the control rods are lifted up and away from the U-235 rods, the fission reaction accelerates and heat is given off. The heat is used to turn water into steam, which turns an electrical turbine generator.

This project will show the four stages of a nuclear reactor in action, using household items.

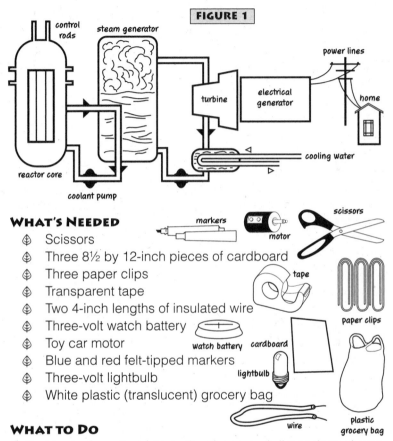

FIGURE 1

control rods
steam generator
power lines
turbine
electrical generator
home
cooling water
reactor core
coolant pump

What's Needed

markers
motor
scissors

⊕ Scissors
⊕ Three 8½ by 12-inch pieces of cardboard
⊕ Three paper clips
⊕ Transparent tape
⊕ Two 4-inch lengths of insulated wire
⊕ Three-volt watch battery
⊕ Toy car motor
⊕ Blue and red felt-tipped markers
⊕ Three-volt lightbulb
⊕ White plastic (translucent) grocery bag

tape
paper clips
watch battery   cardboard
lightbulb
wire
plastic grocery bag

What to Do

Cut a piece of cardboard into the shape and dimensions shown in **Figure 2**. Be sure to cut the slits in the corners.

Bend two paper clips into an **S** shape and tape them to the center of the board. See **Figure 3**.

Strip the insulation from the ends of the two wires and tape one on each side of the watch battery, as shown in **Figure 4**.

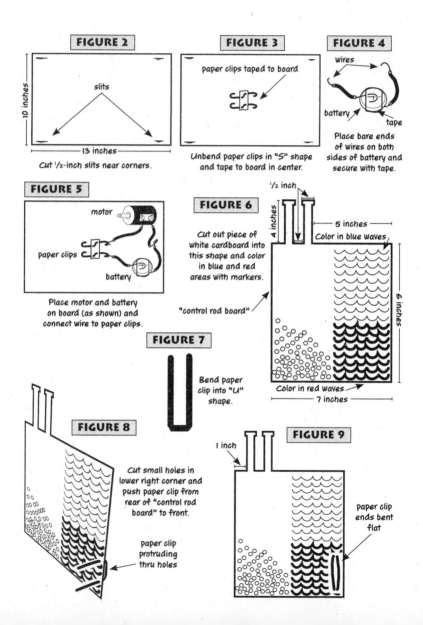

FIGURE 2

10 inches

13 inches

slits

Cut ½-inch slits near corners.

FIGURE 3

paper clips taped to board

Unbend paper clips in "S" shape
and tape to board in center.

FIGURE 4

wires

battery

tape

Place bare ends
of wires on both
sides of battery and
secure with tape.

FIGURE 5

motor

paper clips

battery

Place motor and battery
on board (as shown) and
connect wire to paper clips.

FIGURE 6

Cut out piece of
white cardboard into
this shape and color
in blue and red
areas with markers.

"control rod board"

½ inch

4 inches

5 inches

Color in blue waves

6 inches

Color in red waves

7 inches

FIGURE 7

Bend paper
clip into "U"
shape.

FIGURE 8

Cut small holes in
lower right corner and
push paper clip from
rear of "control rod
board" to front.

paper clip
protruding
thru holes

FIGURE 9

1 inch

paper clip
ends bent
flat

Next, position the battery and motor on the cardboard. Connect the wires in a series from the paper clips to the motor to the battery, as shown in **Figure 5**.

Cut out the second piece of cardboard in the shape and dimensions shown in **Figure 6**. Notice the control rod "handles" at the top. Draw the neutron chain reaction onto the cardboard to represent the U-235 atom fission process of electrons bombarding other atoms, splitting them, and continuing the chain reaction: on the right side of the cardboard, draw blue water waves on the top half and red water waves on the bottom. The red shows the steamy, hot water from the heating process.

Next, bend a paper clip into a **U** shape. See **Figure 7**. Cut small holes in the control rod board's right corner area (the same corner as your red water waves). Push the paper clip through the holes from the back and bend the ends flat. See **Figures 8** and **9**.

When the control rod board is positioned properly on the main board, the "red water wave" paper clip will contact the other two paper clips and complete the electrical circuit, activating the motor. See **Figure 10**.

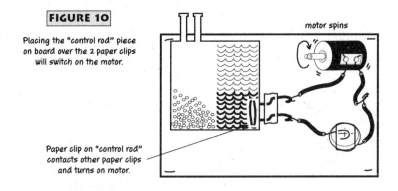

| FIGURE 10 |

Placing the "control rod" piece on board over the 2 paper clips will switch on the motor.

motor spins

Paper clip on "control rod" contacts other paper clips and turns on motor.

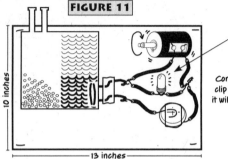

FIGURE 11

3-volt light

Connect 3-volt lightbulb to paper
clip and battery wire as shown so
it will turn on along with the motor.

10 inches

13 inches

Next, connect the light's wires across the motor's wires so it
will turn on with the motor. See **Figure 11**.

Cut two strips of spare cardboard and tape them to the
sides of the control rod board, to ensure that it slides in a
straight path. See **Figure 12**.

Next, cut a piece of cardboard into the dimensions and
shape shown in **Figure 13**. Notice the tabs on each corner.
They will later fit into the main board's corner slots. Also cut
out sections for the reactor core, steam generator, electrical
generator (motor), and house window. Turn the cover board
over, and cut out and tape white translucent plastic over the
cutout sections.

Last, insert the cover board's tabs into the main board's
slots and test to see if all three boards fit properly. Test the
movement of the control rod board to ensure that it will activate
the motor and light. See **Figure 14**.

When all of the sections fit and work properly, sliding the
control rod up will show the reactor core's nuclear fission chain
reaction, which generates steam and turns the turbine. This
activates the electrical generator and distributes power to light
the house. See **Figure 15**.

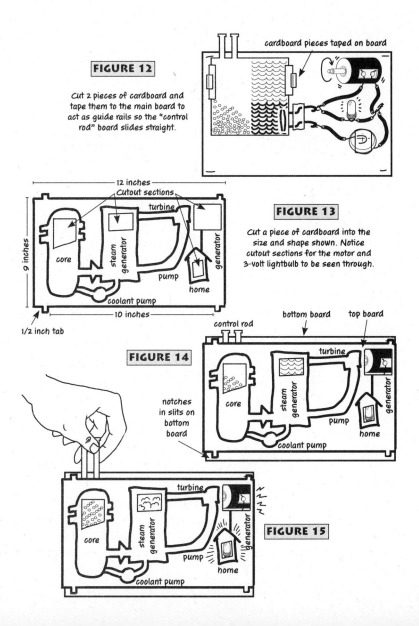

FIGURE 12

Cut 2 pieces of cardboard and tape them to the main board to act as guide rails so the "control rod" board slides straight.

cardboard pieces taped on board

12 inches

Cutout sections

turbine

FIGURE 13

Cut a piece of cardboard into the size and shape shown. Notice cutout sections for the motor and 3-volt lightbulb to be seen through.

9 inches

core

steam generator

pump

generator

home

coolant pump

10 inches

1/2 inch tab

control rod

bottom board

top board

FIGURE 14

notches in slits on bottom board

turbine

core

steam generator

pump

generator

home

coolant pump

turbine

core

steam generator

pump

generator

home

FIGURE 15

coolant pump

PART II

SNEAKY PRODUCT REUSE PROJECTS

You can do more with less. Simple everyday items like paper, cardboard, paper clips, aluminum foil, or paper cups can be quickly transformed into practical projects.

If you're curious about the sneaky adaptation possibilities of more complex household devices, you're in the right place. People frequently throw away damaged gadgets and toys without realizing they can be reused in yet-to-be-discovered ways. For example, according to the American Forest and Paper Association, only 51 percent of the total paper used in the United States is recycled. Yet, even the most common item, like paper, can be reused to make crafts and science toys.

You'll learn sneaky sources for wire and how to connect things. You'll see how to make: a Frisbee disc with ordinary paper; clever center-of-gravity balancing designs; a handheld and a palm-sized cardboard boomerang; a sneaky periscope from a cookie box, and much more.

All of the projects can be made in no time. If you want to practice recycling and learn high-tech resourcefulness, the following projects will provide plenty of fun product-reuse applications.

After absorbing the reuse projects in this chapter undoubtedly new innovative ideas will sneak up on you.

SNEAKY WIRE SOURCES

Ordinary wire can be used in many sneaky ways. You'll soon learn how it can be utilized to make a radio transmitter, a speaker, and more.

When wire is required for sneaky projects, whenever possible try to use everyday items that you might otherwise have thrown away. Recycling metal will help save our natural resources.

Getting Wired

In an emergency, you can obtain wire—or items that can be used as wire—from some very unlikely sources. **Figure 1** illustrates just a few of the possible items that you can use in case connecting wire is not available.

Ready-to-use wire can be obtained from:
   Telephone cords
   TV/VCR cables
   Headphone wire
   Earphone wire
   Speaker wire
   Wire from inside toys, radios, and other electrical devices

Note: Some of the sources above will have one to six separate wires inside.

Wire for projects can also be made from:
   Take-out food container handles
   Twist-ties
   Paper clips

Envelope clasps
Ballpoint pen springs
Fast-food wrappers
Potato chip bag liners

You can also use aluminum from the following items:
Margarine wrappers
Ketchup and condiment packages
Breath mint container labels
Chewing gum wrappers
Trading card packaging
Coffee creamer container lids

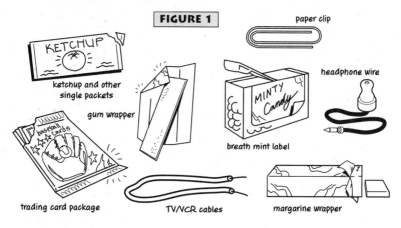

FIGURE 1

paper clip

ketchup and other
single packets

gum wrapper

breath mint label

headphone wire

trading card package

TV/VCR cables

margarine wrapper

Note: The wire used from the sources above are only to be used for low-voltage, battery-powered projects.

Use special care when handling fragile aluminum materials. In some instances, aluminum may be coated with a wax or plastic coating that you may be able to remove.

You can cut strips of aluminum material from food wrappers easily enough. With smaller items—such as aluminum obtained from a coffee cream container—use the sneaky cutting pattern shown in **Figure 2**.

Making resourceful use of items to make sneaky wire is not only intriguing, it's fun.

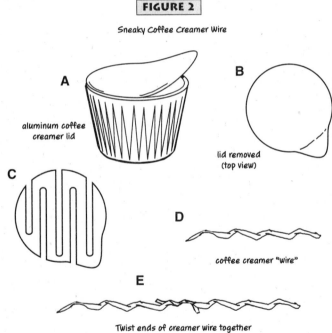

FIGURE 2

Sneaky Coffee Creamer Wire

A

aluminum coffee
creamer lid

B

lid removed
(top view)

C

D

coffee creamer "wire"

E

Twist ends of creamer wire together
for longer runs.

HOW TO CONNECT THINGS

The "Getting Wired" project illustrated how to obtain wire from everyday things. Now you'll learn how to connect the wires to provide consistent performance. (A tight connection is crucial to the operation of electrical projects, otherwise faulty and erratic results may occur.)

Figure 1 shows a piece of insulated wire. The insulation material must be stripped away to make a metal-to-metal connection to other electrical parts. Strip away about one to two inches of insulation from both ends of the wire. See **Figure 2**.

To connect the wire to another wire lead, wrap both ends around each other, as shown in **Figure 3**.

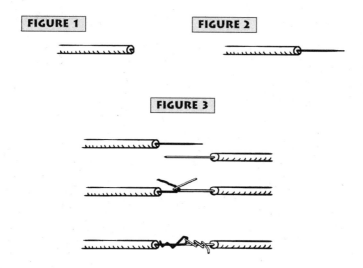

When connecting the wire to the end of a stiff lead (such as the end of an LED), wrap the wire around the lead and bend the lead back over the wire. See **Figure 4**.

To connect wire to the end of a small battery, bend the wire into a circular shape, place it on the battery terminal, and wrap the connection tightly with tape, as shown in **Figure 5**.

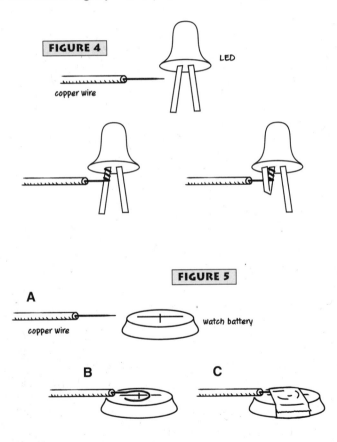

TUBE SORTER

A sneaky item sorter can easily be put together with cardboard tubes and tissue containers that would otherwise be discarded. When covered with gift wrap or color comics pages, it'll make a unique desktop accessory.

What's Needed
- Cardboard tubes, from toilet paper rolls or paper towel rolls
- Paper or plastic tissue dispenser
- Scissors

Optional:
- Tape
- Rubber band
- Wrapping paper

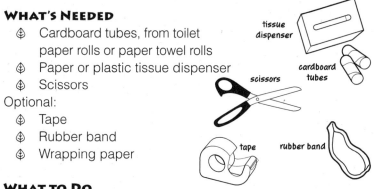

What to Do
Cut off the top of the tissue dispenser, as shown in **Figure 1**. Then, place the cardboard rolls inside the box vertically. You can make an interesting display by cutting the rolls to different lengths and placing the taller ones in the center or rear. See **Figure 2**. If desired, use tape or a rubber band to affix the rolls firmly together.

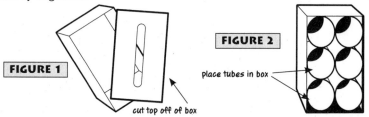

FIGURE 1

cut top off of box

FIGURE 2

place tubes in box

Place your desktop items, like pens, pencils, scissors, etc., inside the rolls as desired. For a pleasing appearance, you can decorate the container with gift-wrap paper or the color comics from the Sunday paper. See **Figure 3**.

If you don't have enough cardboard rolls, rolled-up postcards taped together will do. See **Figure 4**.

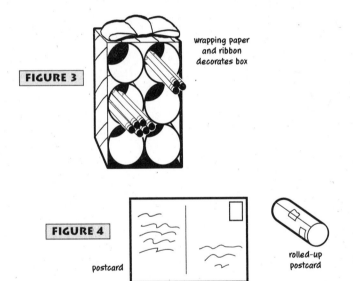

FIGURE 3

wrapping paper
and ribbon
decorates box

FIGURE 4

postcard

rolled-up
postcard

when rolled up and taped, a postcard acts as a tube

SNEAKY REUSABLE CUP WRAPS

If we're prepared, we can do so much better at conserving our daily level of disposable product-packaging consumption. Although most people know the importance of using reusable shopping bags, there are other frequently discarded items that can also be addressed with sneaky substitutes.

If you drink hot chocolate or coffee and dislike unnecessary product-packaging waste, this project is for you: Avoid using and discarding cardboard cup wrappers and make your own sneaky reusable insulator that doubles as an eco-bracelet or armband.

WHAT'S NEEDED

- Old sock or armband
- Scissors
- Velcro dots

WHAT TO DO

Instead of accepting and using a cardboard cup wrap, stretch an armband around the cup instead. Or, simply cut a piece of an old, clean sock into a 1½-inch elastic band as shown in **Figure 1**.

When ordering a hot drink, ask the server not to use a disposable wrap on the cup. Instead, stretch your Sneaky Cup Wrap around the container and remember to remove it when you've finished your beverage. See **Figure 2**.

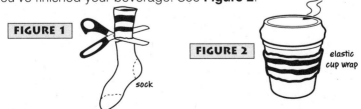

FIGURE 1 — sock

FIGURE 2 — elastic cup wrap

SNEAKY ECO-WRISTBAND

All you need is some spare denim material and Velcro and you
can make a versatile wristband that doubles as a cup insulator.

WHAT'S NEEDED

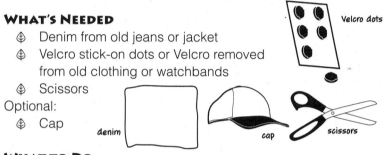

- Denim from old jeans or jacket
- Velcro stick-on dots or Velcro removed
  from old clothing or watchbands
- Scissors

Optional:
- Cap

WHAT TO DO

Cut a piece of denim material into the shape and dimensions
as follows: The bottom length should be 9 inches, the top 11
inches, and the width, approximately 2 inches. See **Figure 3**.

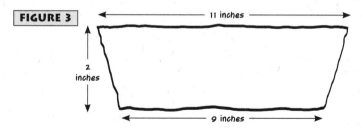

Apply Velcro at each end of the wrap as shown in **Figure 4**.
Now wrap it around your wrist and press it together for a snug
fit. Do not use an insulator wrap on your next hot drink. Simply
remove the sneaky wrap from your arm and attach it to the cup
as shown in **Figure 5**.

SNEAKY REUSABLE CUP WRAPS

If we're prepared, we can do so much better at conserving our daily level of disposable product-packaging consumption. Although most people know the importance of using reusable shopping bags, there are other frequently discarded items that can also be addressed with sneaky substitutes.

If you drink hot chocolate or coffee and dislike unnecessary product-packaging waste, this project is for you: Avoid using and discarding cardboard cup wrappers and make your own sneaky reusable insulator that doubles as an eco-bracelet or armband.

WHAT'S NEEDED

⊕ Old sock or armband
⊕ Scissors
⊕ Velcro dots

Velcro dots

sock

scissors

WHAT TO DO

Instead of accepting and using a cardboard cup wrap, stretch an armband around the cup instead. Or, simply cut a piece of an old, clean sock into a 1½-inch elastic band as shown in **Figure 1**.

When ordering a hot drink, ask the server not to use a disposable wrap on the cup. Instead, stretch your Sneaky Cup Wrap around the container and remember to remove it when you've finished your beverage. See **Figure 2**.

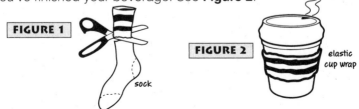

FIGURE 1

sock

FIGURE 2

elastic
cup wrap

SNEAKY ECO-WRISTBAND

All you need is some spare denim material and Velcro and you can make a versatile wristband that doubles as a cup insulator.

What's Needed

Velcro dots

- Denim from old jeans or jacket
- Velcro stick-on dots or Velcro removed from old clothing or watchbands
- Scissors

Optional:

- Cap

denim

cap

scissors

What to Do

Cut a piece of denim material into the shape and dimensions as follows: The bottom length should be 9 inches, the top 11 inches, and the width, approximately 2 inches. See **Figure 3**.

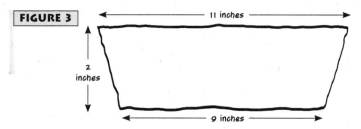

FIGURE 3

11 inches

2 inches

9 inches

Apply Velcro at each end of the wrap as shown in **Figure 4**. Now wrap it around your wrist and press it together for a snug fit. Do not use an insulator wrap on your next hot drink. Simply remove the sneaky wrap from your arm and attach it to the cup as shown in **Figure 5**.

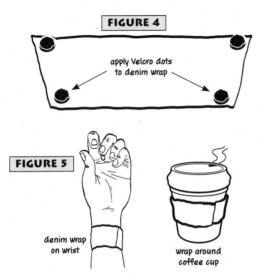

FIGURE 4

apply Velcro dots
to denim wrap

FIGURE 5

denim wrap
on wrist

wrap around
coffee cup

If you don't want to wear the sneaky insulator around your arm, it can be attached to a favorite cap with Velcro applied on the front. See **Figure 6**.

The denim cup wrap can also be stored on the sleeve of a jacket, as shown in **Figure 7**.

The eco-wristband can even hold a spare grocery bag when needed. Neatly fold and compress a plastic grocery bag into a compact square, and secure it with a mini rubber band to the armband as shown in **Figure 8**.

Remove the eco-wristband and wrap it around the cup. Then whenever you need a bag, just take the rubber band off the wristband and unfold the spare plastic bag. See **Figure 9**.

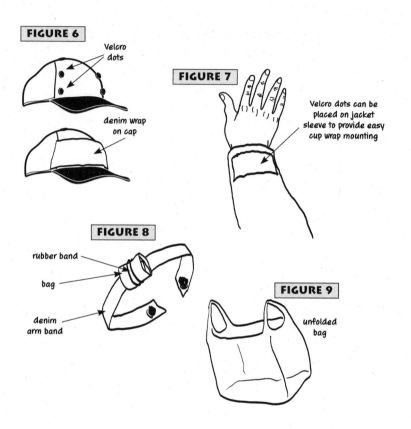

FIGURE 6

Velcro dots

denim wrap on cap

FIGURE 7

Velcro dots can be placed on jacket sleeve to provide easy cup wrap mounting

FIGURE 8

rubber band

bag

denim arm band

FIGURE 9

unfolded bag

SNEAKY GREEN TIP SHEET
AND REMINDER CARD

Although we try to be conscious of "green" living habits, we may not remember all of the best tips. Or, when we spread the message of conservation, people may not remember all of the tips we share.

Make green tip sheets to place on your refrigerator door or for work (or school) and to give away to others.

WHAT'S NEEDED

- Thick paper
- Pen
- Magnet

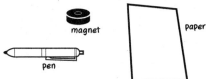

WHAT TO DO

Write (or photocopy) the smart-shopping reminder tips, shown below, on thick paper. Then, place a magnet on top of it to hold it in place on your refrigerator door. Create extra cards and give them to friends and relatives, classmates, and co-workers.

GREEN TIP SHEET

- **Plan your shopping trips in advance. Make a list of what you need. Call a friend to go with you to save fuel (or request to go with them on their trips).**

- Select cleaning products without unnecessary chemicals and excess packaging. Better yet, make your own cleaners with ideas from the Sneaky Cleaners You Can Make section at the end of the book.

- Purchase large quantities to reduce the need for frequent trips, reduce product-packaging waste, and save money.

- Bring your own reusable bags.

- Make the most of your excursions: If you do additional errands when you're out, you'll also save fuel.

You can create tip sheets of various sizes to give to friends and coworkers as desired.

SNEAKY GREEN TIP DISPLAY CASE

Plastic CD and DVD cases aren't just for storing audio/video material. They can act as a nice desktop display for your green tip sheets.

WHAT'S NEEDED

- Green tip sheet
- CD case
- Tape

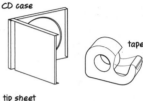

tip sheet

WHAT TO DO

Remove the CD's sleeve notes and replace them with a tip sheet trimmed to fit inside. Open the case to a 45-degree angle and secure it with tape, as shown in **Figure 1**.

Since the tip sheet now takes the place of the CD liner, you can place the display upright on a shelf or table where it can be seen in your home or office. See **Figure 2**.

If you have lots of extra CD cases, you can set up an array that displays various tips or an artistic sequential display, as shown in **Figure 3**.

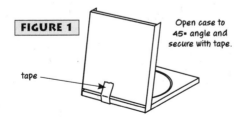

FIGURE 1

Open case to 45° angle and secure with tape.

tape

FIGURE 2

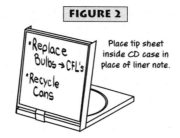

Place tip sheet inside CD case in place of liner note.

FIGURE 3

Sequential picture show on shelf.

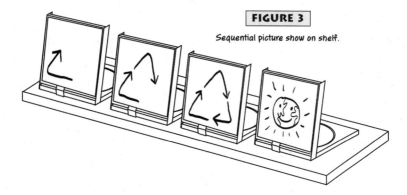

SNEAKY GREEN ECO-HAT

For some of us our hat is a near-constant companion. Why not make it a tool in your eco-arsenal? You can add quite a few conservation tools to a typical baseball cap with a few simple modifications.

WHAT'S NEEDED

- Cap
- Denim or other cloth material that matches cap
- Velcro
- Scissors

Optional eco items:

- Mini tire gauge
- Mini-light
- Mini solar charger (for batteries and cell phone)
- Collapsible cup
- Green fact sheet cards to give away
- Plastic grocery bag
- Small rubber band

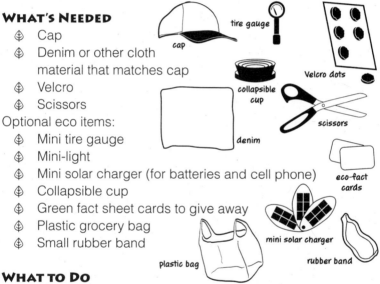

tire gauge

cap

Velcro dots

collapsible cup

scissors

denim

eco-fact cards

mini solar charger

plastic bag

rubber band

WHAT TO DO

Place Velcro on the eco-accessories and place matching Velcro pieces on the front of the cap as shown in **Figure 1**. Then press the eco-accessories on the front of the cap. Fold the grocery bag into a compact square and wrap it with a small rubber band before positioning it on the front of the cap. See **Figure 2**.

Cut the cloth material to a size that matches the outer band of the cap. Affix the small Velcro pieces to the cloth as shown in **Figure 3**.

Last, cover the sneaky eco-accessories with the cloth material for a neat appearance. The optional solar charger can be mounted on the top of the cap with Velcro if desired. See **Figure 4**. This will allow you to charge batteries as you walk.

Now, you can check your friend's tire pressure, give away conservation fact sheets, and have other conservation tools available at a moment's notice.

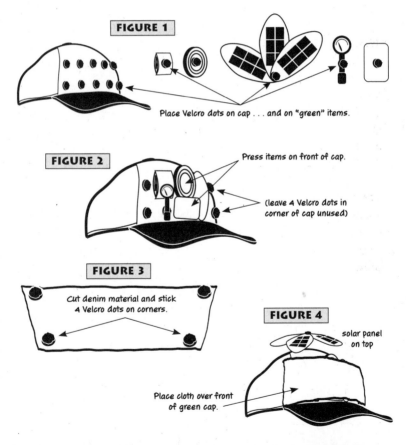

FIGURE 1

Place Velcro dots on cap . . . and on "green" items.

FIGURE 2

Press items on front of cap.

(leave 4 Velcro dots in corner of cap unused)

FIGURE 3

Cut denim material and stick 4 Velcro dots on corners.

FIGURE 4

solar panel on top

Place cloth over front of green cap.

SNEAKY GREEN SNACK KIT

The next time you go to a fast-food restaurant, notice how much excess wrapping paper and plastic is used and then discarded.

Now, multiply the amount of waste that takes place in a month or year. With a little preparation, you can prevent using so much paper and plastic by bringing your own green snack kit.

WHAT'S NEEDED

- Small towel or napkins made from recycled paper
- Collapsible cup
- Cup wrap
- Cinnamon sticks
- Reusable plastic utensils
- Plastic Ziploc bag

WHAT TO DO

On a typical visit to a fast-food restaurant you might use and discard a variety of the following items: a paper cup, plastic cup lid, napkins, a cup wrap, coffee stirrer, and plastic utensils. See **Figure 1**.

| FIGURE 1 | Typical items used once and discarded for a typical coffee or snack. |

Instead, prepare a green snack kit by storing recycled napkins or a small towel, a collapsible cup, a sneaky cup wrap, cinnamon sticks—or a similar edible item to substitute for a coffee stirrer—and plastic utensils in a Ziploc bag. See **Figure 2**.

After your snack, wipe off the cup and utensils and store the items in the Ziploc bag until you can clean them. See **Figure 3**.

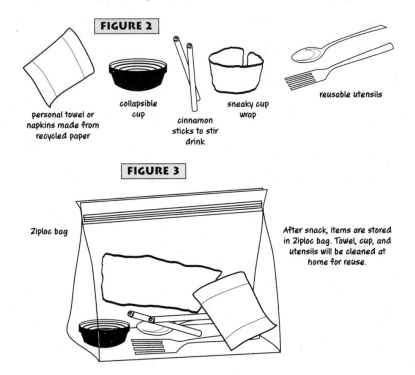

FIGURE 2

personal towel or
napkins made from
recycled paper

collapsible
cup

cinnamon
sticks to stir
drink

sneaky cup
wrap

reusable utensils

FIGURE 3

Ziploc bag

After snack, items are stored
in Ziploc bag. Towel, cup, and
utensils will be cleaned at
home for reuse.

SNEAKY GREEN VEST

For serious eco-warriors, a common vest can act as a portable sneaky storage center for all of your green tools. Compared to the Sneaky Green Eco-Hat, the Sneaky Green Vest can comfortably store more of your green tools—and larger quantities, too.

In addition to the cup wrap and sneaky snack kit, your sneaky eco-vest can store larger items like a full-size tire gauge, green fact sheets, and solar and crank chargers (that allow you to use a revolving crank to charge batteries when a solar charger is not viable).

WHAT'S NEEDED

- Sturdy vest
- Tire gauge
- Mini solar charger for batteries and cell phone
- Mini cranking charger
- Green fact sheet cards to give away
- Plastic bag

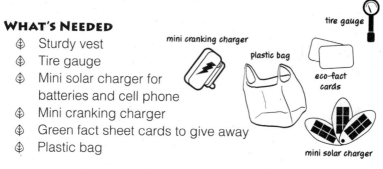

WHAT TO DO

Select a sturdy vest made of durable fabric with large pockets. Lay out your eco-accessories and place them in the vest pockets based on their size, weight, and accessibility as needed.

Figure 1 illustrates a typical vest with the eco-items evenly distributed for comfort and ease of access.

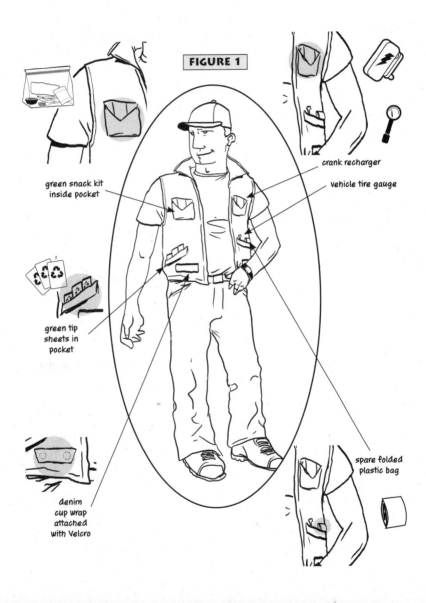

FIGURE 1

green snack kit
inside pocket

crank recharger

vehicle tire gauge

green tip
sheets in
pocket

denim
cup wrap
attached
with Velcro

spare folded
plastic bag

CEREAL/FOOD BOX MAGAZINE AND FILE HOLDER

If you thought the only use for a cereal box is to hold a breakfast treat, think again.

It's a waste to discard large cardboard food boxes when they can act as a periodical container. Add some discarded gift-wrap paper and you can make all sorts of decorative vertical holders for your books, magazines, and personal records.

WHAT'S NEEDED

⚜ Large food box
⚜ Scissors
Optional:
⚜ Wrapping paper and tape

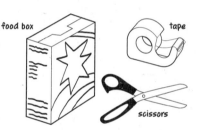

WHAT TO DO

Draw a curved, dipping line on the sides and end of the box as shown in **Figure 1**. Carefully cut along the line and remove the top and sides of the box. See **Figure 2**.

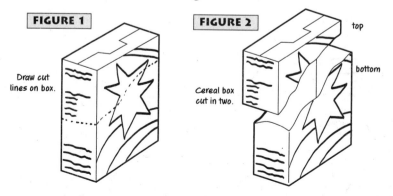

FIGURE 1

Draw cut lines on box.

FIGURE 2

top

bottom

Cereal box cut in two.

Simply place your personal papers or magazines in the box and place it so the spines can be seen. See **Figure 3**.

Optionally, use tape to decorate the sides of the boxes to match the room decor.

FIGURE 3

MAGAZINE DISPLAY RACK

A magazine display rack can be made using corrugated cardboard. This rack has a pleasing angled appearance and allows the magazine cover to be seen face out.

WHAT'S NEEDED

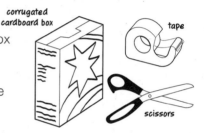

corrugated
cardboard box

tape

scissors

   ☙ Corrugated cardboard box
   ☙ Scissors or cutting tool
Optional:
   ☙ Wrapping paper and tape

WHAT TO DO

Cut two pieces of cardboard, 12 inches long and 8 inches wide, as shown in **Figure 4**. Cut a slot at the middle of the length that extends halfway across the two pieces. Then slide piece **B** into the slots in piece **A**. See **Figure 5**.

    You can cover the cardboard with decorative wrapping paper if desired and then place your magazines on top, as shown in **Figure 6**.

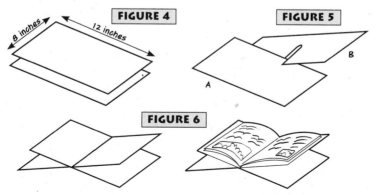

FIGURE 4

8 inches

12 inches

FIGURE 5

B

A

FIGURE 6

REDUCE POST-IT NOTE USAGE

You don't have to be a genius to reuse, and reuse again, normally discarded materials.

3M Company says that Post-it notes account for over a billion dollars in sales. An estimated 1 trillion Post-it notes have been sold nationally since they were first introduced in 1980.

Any method to reuse this popular item is welcome. You can apply the following few tips and then tell others about them.

WHAT'S NEEDED
- Post-it note
- Light pen
- Dark pen
- Pencil

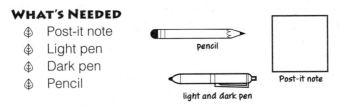

pencil

Post-it note

light and dark pen

WHAT TO DO
First, after writing on one side of a Post-it note, simply bend up the note so you'll be reminded to use the reverse side. See **Figure 1**.

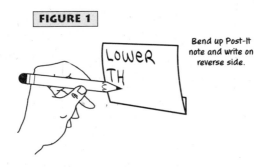

FIGURE 1

LOWER
TH

Bend up Post-It note and write on reverse side.

Second, use a pencil when writing messages so the note can be reused multiple times. Or, if you prefer, use a light-colored pen when writing the first message and then a dark-colored one for the next one. This way you can use the Post-it multiple times before discarding it. See **Figure 2**.

Third, use the adhesive of a used Post-it note to stick up blank paper from junk mail to use as a new note as shown in **Figure 3**.

FIGURE 2

First message written in light colored pen.

Buy milk

Set alarm for meeting

Second message with dark ink or marker.

FIGURE 3

piece of used Post-It note

Set alarm tonight

Let the cat in tonight

paper

SNEAKY BOOK SAFE

Reread a book? We all do it. Reuse a book? It may seem strange at first, but you can make use of an unneeded title in imaginative ways.

If you're not going to give your books away to local libraries and organizations (which is always a good idea), you can make use of them for a sneaky purpose.

WHAT'S NEEDED

- ⊕ Old hardcover book that's at least two hundred pages
- ⊕ Scissors
- ⊕ Pencil
- ⊕ Gluestick

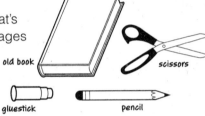

old book

scissors

gluestick

pencil

WHAT TO DO

A thick hardcover book is preferred for this project. It provides ample room for a secret compartment for your valuables.

With a pencil, mark a square segment in the middle of one of the center pages. Do not use the first or last fifty pages in case someone examines the book. See **Figure 1**.

FIGURE 1

Mark square segment to cut on center pages.

Carefully cut out the square shape from one hundred or more middle pages in order to provide a ½-inch to 1-inch compartment for your secret item. Once your item is in place, apply glue stick to the bottom of the last non-cut page and on top of the first cut-away page and press firmly, as shown in **Figure 2**. Also, apply glue stick to the bottom of the last cut page and on top of the next non-cut page and press securely. This prevents the item from being seen or falling out when moved.

Now, you can be secure an item in (almost) plain sight is safe and that you have reused a book for another purpose. See **Figure 3**.

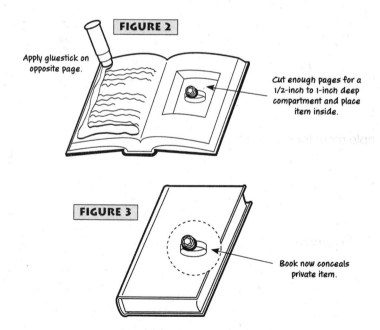

FIGURE 2

Apply gluestick on opposite page.

Cut enough pages for a 1/2-inch to 1-inch deep compartment and place item inside.

FIGURE 3

Book now conceals private item.

SNEAKY ANIMATED ORIGAMI

Paper folding is fun but you can enhance your enjoyment by making the following sneaky origami designs that include motion action using everyday things.

SNEAKY HEAD-BOBBING BIRD

WHAT'S NEEDED
- Scissors
- Paper
- Pencil

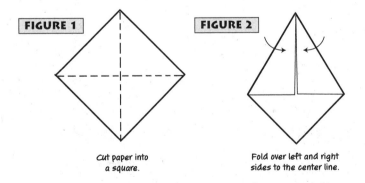

WHAT TO DO
Cut the paper into a square and fold/unfold both the diagonals, as shown in **Figure 1**. Fold over the top left and right corners to the center. See **Figure 2**.

FIGURE 1

Cut paper into
a square.

FIGURE 2

Fold over left and right
sides to the center line.

Then, fold over the lower left and right corners toward the center as shown in **Figure 3**. Fold up the bottom point to the center line to form a tail and fold the top corner toward the back of the figure to make the head, as shown in **Figures 4** and **5**.

Next, fold the figure in half vertically along the center toward the tail. This will bend the tail and head outward as shown in **Figure 6**. Draw eyes and a beak on the figure as desired.

Last, with the sneaky bird standing upright, push down on the center of the tail. The head should move downward. See **Figure 7**.

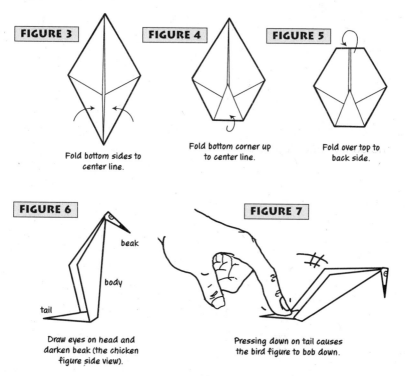

FIGURE 3

Fold bottom sides to center line.

FIGURE 4

Fold bottom corner up to center line.

FIGURE 5

Fold over top to back side.

FIGURE 6

beak

body

tail

Draw eyes on head and darken beak (the chicken figure side view).

FIGURE 7

Pressing down on tail causes the bird figure to bob down.

SNEAKY MOUTH FLAPPER

WHAT'S NEEDED

- ⊕ Scissors
- ⊕ Paper
- ⊕ Pencil

WHAT TO DO

Cut the paper into a square, as shown in **Figure 1**. Next, fold and unfold the square on both the diagonals. Fold over the lower left and right corners to the center. See **Figure 2**.

Then, fold over the upper left and right corners toward the center, as shown in **Figure 3**. Fold up the bottom half of the figure along the center crease. See **Figure 4**. Fold down the top front corner to the bottom of the figure, as shown in **Figure 5**.

Fold the top back tip down and to the left along the fold line shown in **Figure 5**. Then, fold the bottom front tip up and to the left along its indicated diagonal fold line, until it resembles the shape in **Figure 6**. Unfold the left-pointing tips back to their positions shown in **Figure 5**. See **Figure 7**.

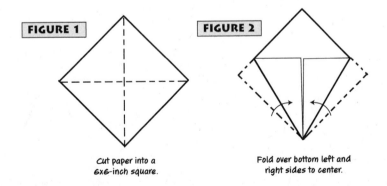

FIGURE 1	FIGURE 2
Cut paper into a 6x6-inch square.	Fold over bottom left and right sides to center.

Next, fold the top corner down and to the right in the opposite direction of how you folded it to make **Figure 6**. Similarly, fold the bottom corner up but to the right, until the shape appears like the one in **Figure 8**.

Fold the bottom right corner to the center—it will fold the figure in half. See **Figure 9**. While you are folding it, shape the top right-pointing corners into a mouth shape by pushing the beak with your hand. See **Figure 10**. If necessary, fold and unfold the figure until this section resembles a mouth.

Last, draw eyes on both sides of the top portion of the figure. Now you can pull on the two bottom corners and the mouth will flap open and close, as shown in **Figure 11**. If not, unfold the beak and refold it while adjusting it with your hand until the mouth moves properly.

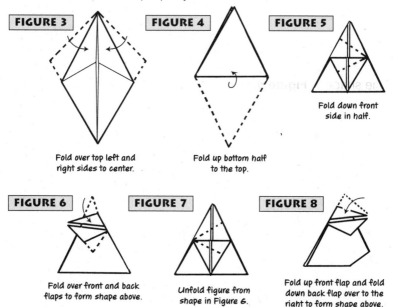

FIGURE 3
Fold over top left and right sides to center.

FIGURE 4
Fold up bottom half to the top.

FIGURE 5
Fold down front side in half.

FIGURE 6
Fold over front and back flaps to form shape above.

FIGURE 7
Unfold figure from shape in Figure 6.

FIGURE 8
Fold up front flap and fold down back flap over to the right to form shape above.

FIGURE 9

Bend bottom right
section to center
and fold.

FIGURE 10

Form top sections
into mouth shape.
If necessary, unfold
and fold bottom section.

FIGURE 11

Pull bottom section
apart and the mouth
will open and close.

SNEAKY ORIGAMI ANIMATOR

You can add motion to your origami designs, and other craft
creations, by making a Sneaky Origami Animator with everyday
objects.

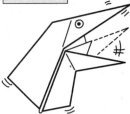

pliers

electrical tape

paper clips

cardboard

WHAT'S NEEDED

- ✤ Two large paper clips
- ✤ Electrical tape
- ✤ Five by three-inch piece of cardboard
- ✤ Needle-nose pliers

WHAT TO DO

This project illustrates how to make a cam-crank toy to add
locomotion to your still figure designs. You can produce variations
on this design by using larger pieces of cardboard and stiff wire,
but it's recommended to make a simple version first. Later, you
can alter the size of the parts to produce your desired results.

First, bend one paper clip into the shape shown in **Figure 1**.
It will act as a mount for your origami figure.

Next, bend the second paper clip into the shape shown in **Figure 2**. It will act as a cranking cam that will move the first paper clip up and down. Wrap electrical tape around both paper clips.

Poke holes in the cardboard at 1-inch, 2½-inch, and 4-inch intervals, as shown in **Figure 3**. Then, stand the card along its long side and fold it into a **U** shape.

Push the first paper clip into the center hole. Use pliers to bend the top of the clip into a **C** shape so it will not fall through the hole. See **Figures 4** and **5**.

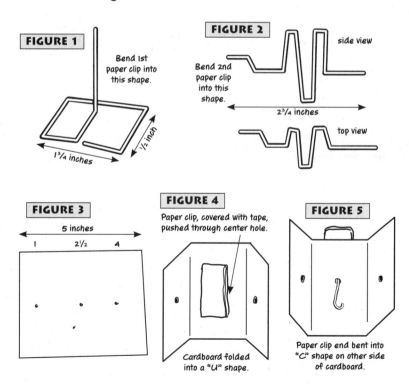

FIGURE 1

Bend 1st paper clip into this shape.

1¾ inches

½ inch

FIGURE 2

Bend 2nd paper clip into this shape.

side view

2¾ inches

top view

FIGURE 3

5 inches

1   2½   4

FIGURE 4

Paper clip, covered with tape, pushed through center hole.

Cardboard folded into a "U" shape.

FIGURE 5

Paper clip end bent into "C" shape on other side of cardboard.

Next, push the second paper clip into the side holes of the cardboard so it rests underneath the first paper clip, as shown in **Figure 6**. Apply tape to the bottom of the cardboard to keep its shape.

Last, turn the paper clip crank on the side of the Sneaky Origami Animator and the top paper clip will move up and down. See **Figure 7**. Since the first paper clip has an irregular shape, it acts as a cam mechanism and causes erratic movement on the other paper clip resting on it.

You can attach small paper figures to the top paper clip with tape. Experiment with an assortment of shapes for your paper clip cam (e.g., oval or triangular shapes) to produce a variety of motion effects. See the moving-arm figure in **Figure 8**.

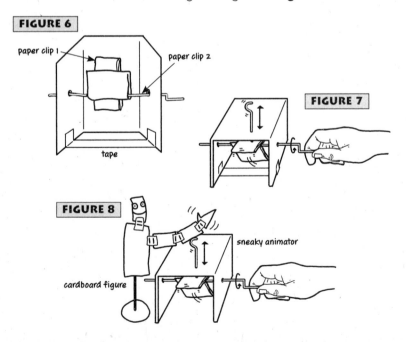

FIGURE 6

paper clip 1
paper clip 2
tape

FIGURE 7

FIGURE 8

sneaky animator
cardboard figure

SNEAKY BOOMERANG

Want a sneaky way to play catch alone? You just need a piece of cardboard and foam rubber to make a working boomerang that will actually fly up to 30 feet away and return.

WHAT'S NEEDED

- ✛ Scissors
- ✛ Cardboard from a food box
- ✛ Foam rubber, from an old pillow
- ✛ Transparent tape

WHAT TO DO

Cut the cardboard into the boomerang shape shown in **Figure 1**. Each wing of the boomerang should be 9 inches long by 2 inches wide.

Then, cut two foam pieces into 6 by 2-inch oval shapes with one side rising into a curve. The rising shape should resemble the side view of an airplane wing. See **Figure 2**. Place the oval foam pieces on the leading edges of the boomerang and secure them with tape.

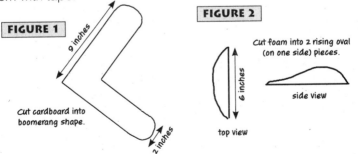

FIGURE 1

9 inches

2 inches

Cut cardboard into boomerang shape.

FIGURE 2

Cut foam into 2 rising oval (on one side) pieces.

6 inches

top view

side view

Note: Look carefully at the placement of the ovals on the boomerang wings in **Figure 3** before taping them. The foam creates a curved shape on the boomerang wing, which will cause air to move faster across its top than across the bottom surface. This will produce lift for the boomerang.

Hold the boomerang as if you were going to throw a baseball and throw it straight overhead (not to the side). See **Figure 4**. The Sneaky Boomerang should fly straight and return to the left. Experiment with different angles of throw to obtain a desired return pattern.

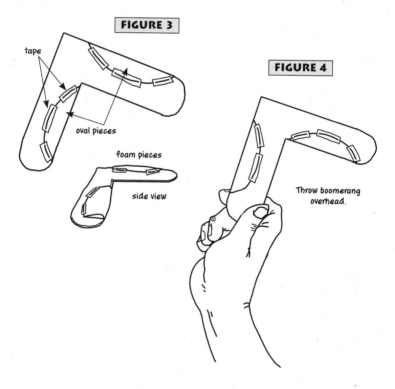

FIGURE 3

tape

oval pieces

foam pieces

side view

FIGURE 4

Throw boomerang overhead.

SNEAKY MINI-BOOMERANG

You can use postcards, business cards, or cardboard food boxes to make a miniature, palm-size boomerang that actually flies and returns to you, for indoor fun.

WHAT'S NEEDED

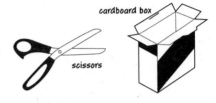

cardboard box

- Scissors
- Cardboard from food boxes or postcards

scissors

WHAT TO DO

Cut out the boomerang shapes shown in **Figure 1**. The boomerang wings can be any length between 2 to 4 inches. For optimal flight height and return performance, cut each wing of the boomerang 2½ inches long and ½ inch wide.

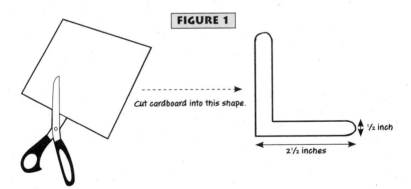

FIGURE 1

Cut cardboard into this shape.

½ inch

2½ inches

Set the Sneaky Mini-Boomerang on the palm of your raised hand with one wing hanging off. Tilt your hand slightly upward. With your other hand's thumb and middle finger ¹/₂ inch away, snap the outer boomerang wing. You'll discover (after a few attempts) that it will fly forward and return to you. See **Figure 2**.

Note: You must snap your finger with a strong snapping action to make the boomerang fly away and return properly, as shown in **Figure 3**.

Experiment with different hand positions and angles to control the boomerang's flight pattern.

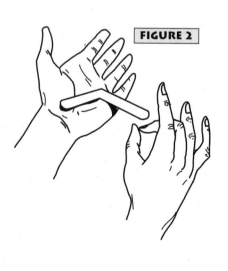

SNEAKY FLYING DISK

Now it's time to make a sneaky flyer, similar to flying disk toys, using paper and tape.

WHAT'S NEEDED

- Scissors
- Paper, 8½ x 11 inches
- Transparent tape

WHAT TO DO

Cut eight 2-inch square pieces of paper as shown in **Figure 1**. Fold the top right corner of one square down to the lower left corner. See **Figure 2**. Then, fold the top left corner down to the bottom, as shown in **Figure 3**.

Repeat these two folds with the remaining seven squares. See **Figure 4**.

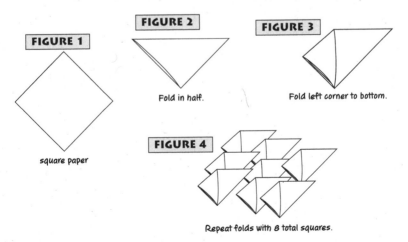

FIGURE 1

square paper

FIGURE 2

Fold in half.

FIGURE 3

Fold left corner to bottom.

FIGURE 4

Repeat folds with 8 total squares.

Insert one paper figure into the left pocket of another, as shown in **Figure 5**. Repeat inserting the figures into one another until they form an eight-sided doughnut shape; see **Figure 6**. Apply tape as needed to keep the origami flyer together and turn over, as shown in **Figure 7**.

Next, bend down the outer edge of the sneaky flyer to form a lip, as shown in **Figure 8**. This outer lip will cause the air to take a longer path over it.

Turn the device so the lip is bent downward. Throw the Sneaky Flying Disk with a quick snap of your wrist and it should stay aloft for a great distance.

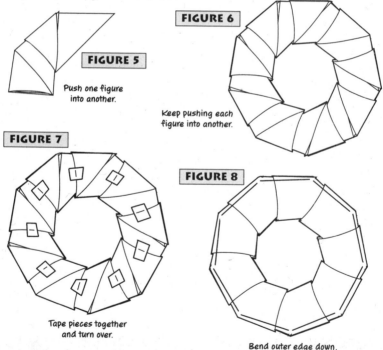

FIGURE 5

Push one figure into another.

FIGURE 6

Keep pushing each figure into another.

FIGURE 7

Tape pieces together and turn over.

FIGURE 8

Bend outer edge down.

PART III

SNEAKY RECYCLING PROJECTS

Recycling is work. Sorting discards can be mundane and tedious. It's easier to just throw away all types of waste in the same trash bin. But there's a way to keep at it and convince others to save our resources: Make it fun.

Here are some sneaky, easy-to-make recycling activities and projects designed to keep you, your friends, and your family motivated. These procedures only require items that you already have around the house. In fact, some of the most versatile items will very likely be found in your garbage can or recycling bin.

Be sure you have extra materials handy: When your friends see your sneaky sorters and unique recycle bins, they will undoubtedly beg you to make versions for them too!

SNEAKY RECYCLE BIN WIRE ADD-ON

Instead of buying extra recycling containers for paper, batteries, and cans, simply adapt an existing trash can into a sneaky sorter. With just an ordinary wire clothes hanger and an extra bag, you can add one to four extra receptacles.

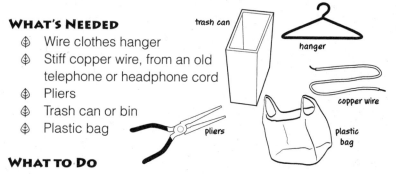

WHAT'S NEEDED
- Wire clothes hanger
- Stiff copper wire, from an old telephone or headphone cord
- Pliers
- Trash can or bin
- Plastic bag

trash can

hanger

copper wire

plastic bag

pliers

WHAT TO DO
In this example a common rectangular trash bin is used that measures 12 inches long by 7 inches wide by 12 inches high. Using the pliers, carefully bend the wire hanger into the shape and dimensions shown in **Figure 1**. Note: The dimensions are approximate since you'll adapt your wire bag holders to your own container's height and width.

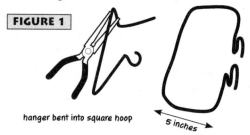

| FIGURE 1 |

hanger bent into square hoop

5 inches

Next, carefully cut three, 18-inch lengths of wire and wrap them around the hanger loop so it forms a support net for the bag as shown in **Figure 2**.

Remove the lid of the trash bin, if applicable, and slip the two curved end clamps over the side. See **Figure 3**. Place a used plastic grocery bag in and around the hanger to hold your recyclables. See **Figure 4**.

The recycle bin can also be mounted in other locations like a car trunk to store beverage bottles, cans, and depleted batteries. A trunk-mounted bin is convenient since when you go to the local recycle center, you can just grab the bag of recyclables from your trunk.

The trunk-mounted add-on bin can be fastened to: an existing brace or metal molding inside the trunk, a storage box, or hung on an existing trunk net. You can also install stick-on hooks as a way of supporting the add-on bin. See **Figures 5** and **6**.

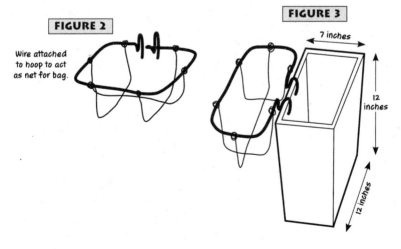

FIGURE 2

Wire attached to hoop to act as net for bag.

FIGURE 3

7 inches

12 inches

12 inches

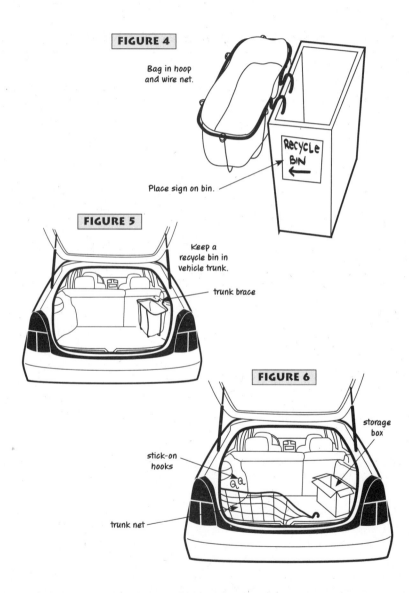

FIGURE 4

Bag in hoop
and wire net.

Place sign on bin.

Recycle BIN

FIGURE 5

Keep a
recycle bin in
vehicle trunk.

trunk brace

FIGURE 6

storage box

stick-on hooks

trunk net

SNEAKY WIRE RECYCLE BIN II

Here's a second method to convert a waste bin into a green recyclable sorter.

WHAT'S NEEDED

- Waste bin
- Wire hangers
- Pliers
- Two plastic bags
- Cardboard
- Eight magnets
- Scissors
- Tape

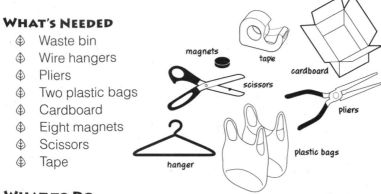

magnets
tape
cardboard
scissors
pliers
plastic bags
hanger

WHAT TO DO

Cut a piece of cardboard into the same length and width as your waste bin. Then cut two square holes in the top. Next, tape four magnets to the corners of the cardboard and to the top of the waste bin. See **Figure 1**.

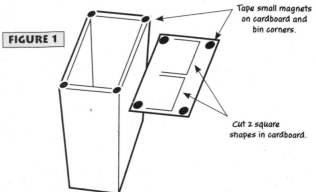

FIGURE 1

Tape small magnets on cardboard and bin corners.

Cut 2 square shapes in cardboard.

Bend a wire hanger into the rectangular shape shown in **Figure 2**. Make sure the two lengths are as long as the width of the waste bin and then place it on top of the bin.

Insert two plastic grocery bags into the bin so they wrap around the wire hanger. See **Figure 3**.

Place the cardboard piece on top and the magnets will keep it in place. Design and tape signs to the side of the bin directing people to discard recyclables in the proper receptacle as shown in **Figure 4**.

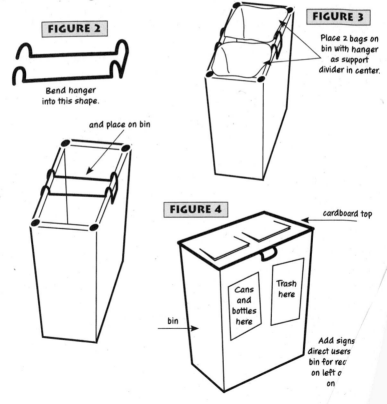

FIGURE 2

Bend hanger
into this shape.

and place on bin

FIGURE 3

Place 2 bags on
bin with hanger
as support
divider in center.

FIGURE 4

cardboard top

Cans
and
bottles
here

Trash
here

bin

Add signs
direct users
bin for rec
on left o
on

SNEAKY RECYCLE BIN

Here's a great way to demonstrate how to rescue and reuse product packaging. You can make great-looking recycling containers for cans, small bottles, and old batteries with cardboard obtained from discarded cereal and cookie boxes and other food containers that would otherwise go into the trash.

These sneaky recycle bins can be used as stand-alone containers or placed inside of multi-item bins that you'll see in upcoming projects.

WHAT'S NEEDED

cereal boxes

- Two large cereal boxes 12 inches tall by 8¼ inches wide and 2¾ inches deep
- Scissors
- Plastic bag
- Marker

marker

plastic bag

scissors

WHAT TO DO

Cut off the top, bottom, and sides of the cereal boxes so the four sections remain that are 12 inches by 8¼ inches. **Figures 1a**, **1b**, and **1c** illustrate the bottom, sides, front, and back pieces of the bin. The bottom piece is rectangular with tabs on all four sides with the following dimensions: 7½ inches long by 5½ inches wide with ½-inch tabs that are ¼ inch deep on all four sides. The two side pieces are 8 inches wide by 5½ inches tall. The side pieces also include notched slits cut into the four corners and in the bottom middle area. It also has a ½-inch tall by 7-inch wide raised-up middle section at its top.

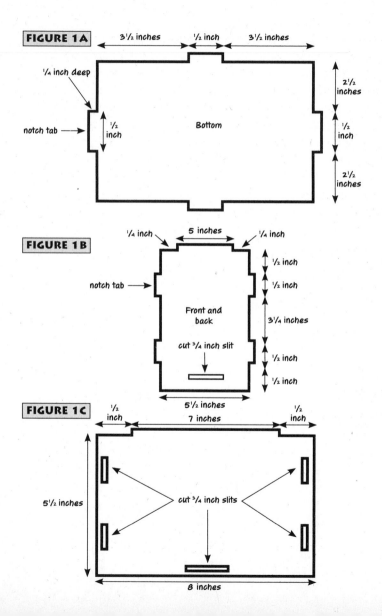

FIGURE 1A

3¹/₂ inches   ¹/₂ inch   3¹/₂ inches

¹/₄ inch deep

notch tab

¹/₂ inch

Bottom

2¹/₂ inches

¹/₂ inch

2¹/₂ inches

FIGURE 1B

¹/₄ inch   5 inches   ¹/₄ inch

notch tab

Front and back

cut ³/₄ inch slit

¹/₂ inch
¹/₂ inch

3¹/₄ inches

¹/₂ inch
¹/₂ inch

5¹/₂ inches

FIGURE 1C

¹/₂ inch   7 inches   ¹/₂ inch

cut ³/₄ inch slits

5¹/₂ inches

8 inches

The dimensions for the front and back sections are as follows: 5¼ inches tall by 5½ inches wide. They have one ¾-inch slit on the bottom, four ½-inch tabs on both sides and a 5¼-inch wide by ¼-inch tall raised section on top.

When assembled, the front and back piece tabs slide into the notches in the side pieces. Similarly, the bottom section's tabs slide into the front, back, and side notches. If necessary, trim the tab pieces for a snug fit. See **Figure 2**.

Once the bin sits upright, bend the tabs back for a secure fit. Place a plastic bag over the top of the bin and use a marker to decorate it as desired. See **Figure 3**.

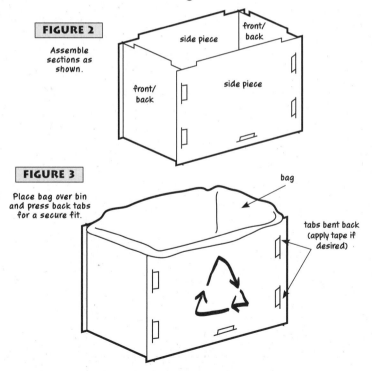

FIGURE 2

Assemble sections as shown.

side piece

front/back

front/back

side piece

FIGURE 3

Place bag over bin and press back tabs for a secure fit.

bag

tabs bent back (apply tape if desired)

SNEAKY RECYCLE MULTI-BIN

This project illustrates how to convert a very large cardboard box into a multi-container recycling bin. The box should be 2 feet long by 1 foot high by ½ foot wide or larger.

What's Needed

- Large corrugated cardboard box
- Four small boxes, approximately 4 inches square
- Scissors or cutting tool
- Plastic bags
- Velcro

Optional:

- Decorative wrapping paper, tape, and markers

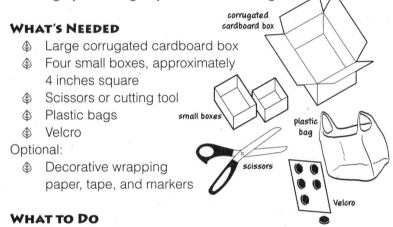

What to Do

Cut off the two short end flaps from the large box as shown in **Figure 1**. Place the box on its side and put the four small boxes inside the large box with their lids folded in. These boxes will hold the recyclable items thrown inside the large bin. See **Figure 2**.

Cut two small, 3-inch by 1-inch rectangular strips from the discarded cardboard flaps and tape Velcro on them as shown in **Figure 3**. Then tape the strips on the large box flaps to act as a door latch. When it's time to empty the small boxes inside, just pull open the flap doors and you have easy access to your recycling. See **Figure 4**.

Cut three sides of a 5-inch square hole to act as a door flap, two on the front, and two more on the top of the large box.

Secure the front flap doors. Test your recycle bin by throwing a soda can inside each square flap, on the top and front of the bin, to be sure it falls into the box inside. If necessary, reposition the small boxes. See **Figures 5** and **6**.

Draw and tape signs on the top and sides of the box directing people where to toss their recyclable discards as shown in **Figure 7**.

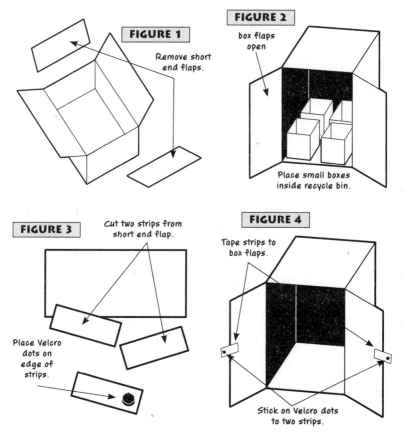

FIGURE 1

Remove short end flaps.

FIGURE 2

box flaps open

Place small boxes inside recycle bin.

FIGURE 3

Cut two strips from short end flap.

Place Velcro dots on edge of strips.

FIGURE 4

Tape strips to box flaps.

Stick on Velcro dots to two strips.

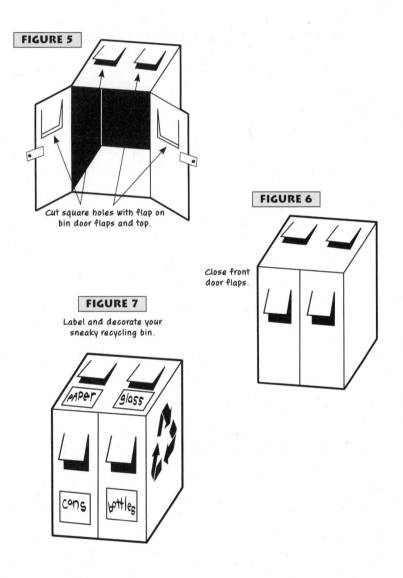

FIGURE 5

Cut square holes with flap on bin door flaps and top.

FIGURE 6

Close front door flaps.

FIGURE 7

Label and decorate your sneaky recycling bin.

paper

glass

cans

bottles

SNEAKY ROBOT RECYCLE BIN

If you used the basic Sneaky Recycle Bin design in the previous project, you can now make one with a fun robot theme.

The head of the robot is simply a smaller box, with a shallow box inside to collect used batteries. The robot's body (the Sneaky Recycle Bin) is mounted on four chip cans that are positioned on top of a wide lower box.

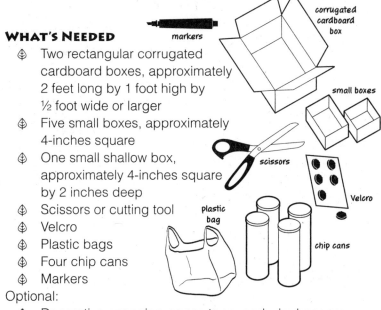

WHAT'S NEEDED

- Two rectangular corrugated cardboard boxes, approximately 2 feet long by 1 foot high by ½ foot wide or larger
- Five small boxes, approximately 4-inches square
- One small shallow box, approximately 4-inches square by 2 inches deep
- Scissors or cutting tool
- Velcro
- Plastic bags
- Four chip cans
- Markers

Optional:

- Decorative wrapping paper, tape, and wire hangers

WHAT TO DO

First, construct a Sneaky Recycle Bin. Then, you will turn one of the small boxes into a mini-bin with a box inside to collect old batteries.

First, remove the side flaps from the boxes as shown in **Figure 1**. Cut a square flap into the side of the small box and place the small, shallow box inside. Place four pieces of Velcro on top of the large bin and on the bottom of the small box and make sure they align properly. Decorate the small box with "eyes" with markers as needed. See **Figure 2**.

Apply four pieces of Velcro to the top of the large bin near the front. You can now use the Velcro to hold the small box on top of the larger one. Also, apply four pieces of Velcro on the large box's bottom near the corners. Then affix the chip cans to the bottom of the bin as shown in **Figure 3**.

Press Velcro on the plastic lids and bottoms of the four chip cans. See **Figure 4**.

Apply four pieces of Velcro to the top of the second large box and press the four chip cans on top. Decorate the front and sides of the box so it resembles robot legs or a tractors' tires and belt as shown in **Figure 5**.

Set the robot body on top of the chip cans and press securely in place. See **Figure 6**. You can decorate the head of the robot with bottle caps, wire, and markers for added effect. See the next section for more sneaky bin accessory tips.

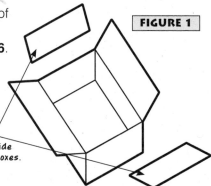

FIGURE 1

Remove side
flaps from boxes.

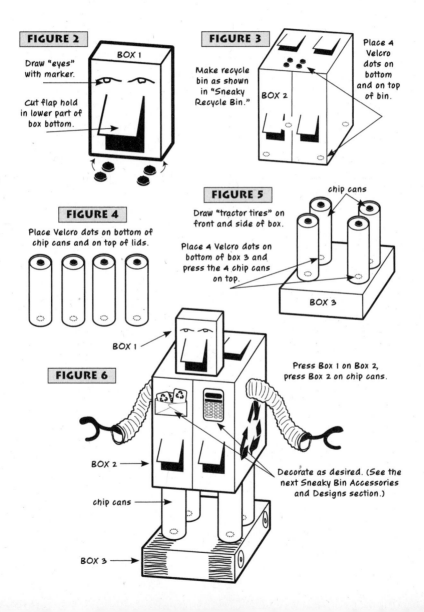

FIGURE 2

BOX 1

Draw "eyes" with marker.

Cut flap hold in lower part of box bottom.

FIGURE 3

Make recycle bin as shown in "Sneaky Recycle Bin."

BOX 2

Place 4 Velcro dots on bottom and on top of bin.

FIGURE 4

Place Velcro dots on bottom of chip cans and on top of lids.

FIGURE 5

chip cans

Draw "tractor tires" on front and side of box.

Place 4 Velcro dots on bottom of box 3 and press the 4 chip cans on top.

BOX 3

FIGURE 6

BOX 1

Press Box 1 on Box 2, press Box 2 on chip cans.

BOX 2

chip cans

Decorate as desired. (See the next Sneaky Bin Accessories and Designs section.)

BOX 3

MORE SNEAKY BIN ACCESSORIES AND DESIGNS

Use items found around the house and decorate your sneaky bin with innovative designs to make it fun to see and use. The techniques in this section will also enable you to create additional innovative sneaky bin accessories to suit your tastes. For instance, at Halloween make a monster bin. At Christmastime, construct a Sneaky Santa Claus container. You can also assemble sneaky bins that resemble your favorite TV and movie characters or props like a futuristic spaceship bin or a spy agency supercomputer recycle bin.

WHAT'S NEEDED

- Large rubber bands
- Envelope
- Velcro
- Small magnets
- Two wire garment hangers
- Slinky toy or flexible tubing hose
- Scissors or cutting tool
- Markers

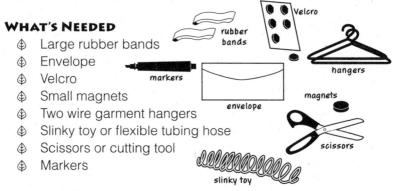

WHAT TO DO

To keep the Sneaky Recycle Multi-Bin door flaps from losing their elasticity, cut a rubber band and tape the ends loosely across the inside as shown in **Figure 1**. Attach a green tips holder with tape to educate users. See **Figure 2**.

Make your sneaky bin adaptable to newer designs and accessories by taping small magnets inside. You can then affix magnets to accessorize and decorate items, like a calculator, and place them on the bins as desired for a fresh appearance. See **Figure 3**.

An ordinary wire garment hanger can be bent into a **C** shape so it resembles a robot arm. Bend the other end of the hanger into a square **U** shape. Cut a slit in the side of the bin to slide the **U** shape of the robot arm into its mounting location. See **Figure 4**. Decorate the robot arm with tubing, or electrical tape and foil as shown in **Figure 5**.

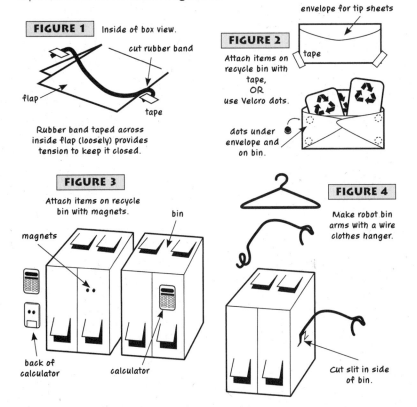

FIGURE 1 Inside of box view.

cut rubber band

flap

tape

Rubber band taped across inside flap (loosely) provides tension to keep it closed.

envelope for tip sheets

FIGURE 2

Attach items on recycle bin with tape, OR use Velcro dots.

tape

dots under envelope and on bin.

FIGURE 3

Attach items on recycle bin with magnets.

magnets

bin

back of calculator

calculator

FIGURE 4

Make robot bin arms with a wire clothes hanger.

Cut slit in side of bin.

Recycle bin flaps don't have to be plain square shapes. For an innovative look, cut them in the shape of the intended recyclable items, like a soda can or two-liter bottle. See **Figure 6**.

Use markers to draw racing stripes, flares, teeth, and creature faces around the bin flaps as shown in **Figure 7**.

Figure 8 illustrates a sneaky race car bin that is constructed similar to the robot but uses a small box attached to the top of a long rectangular box. Flaps are cut on the car's roof, hood, and trunk.

A sneaky rocket bin is made easily enough with one large box, a piece of cardboard folded into a nose cone on top, and a cardboard "stand" acting as rocket fins. See **Figure 9**.

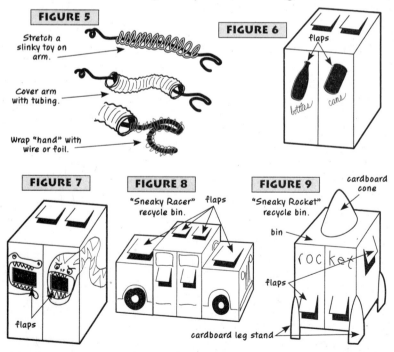

FIGURE 5

Stretch a slinky toy on arm.

Cover arm with tubing.

Wrap "hand" with wire or foil.

FIGURE 6

flaps

bottles   cans

FIGURE 7

flaps

FIGURE 8

"Sneaky Racer" recycle bin.

flaps

FIGURE 9

cardboard cone

"Sneaky Rocket" recycle bin.

bin

rocket

flaps

cardboard leg stand

SNEAKY SHELF

In this project you'll construct a three-level shelf using items you would likely throw away. It can also be converted into a two-level version depending on your needs.

WHAT'S NEEDED

- ⚘ Six chip cans
- ⚘ Velcro
- ⚘ Three plastic utility part boxes, approximately 12 inches by 5 inches by 1 inch deep
- ⚘ Four long, strong rubber bands

Optional:

- ⚘ Wrapping paper and tape

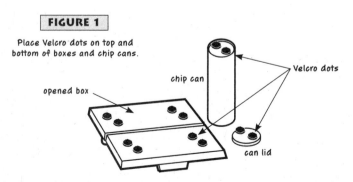

chip cans

Velcro

rubber bands

utility part boxes

WHAT TO DO

Apply Velcro on the top and bottom of the utility part boxes and on the top and bottom of the chip cans so they match each other. See **Figure 1**.

FIGURE 1

Place Velcro dots on top and bottom of boxes and chip cans.

opened box

chip can

Velcro dots

can lid

Next, attach the chip cans to each end of the part boxes and press firmly so the Velcro holds them in place. Place rubber bands on each end of the boxes to keep them secure. See **Figure 2**.

The shelf height can be lowered by unlatching the second box from the top's latch and folding it back as shown in **Figure 3**.

If desired, decorate the shelf and cans with interesting wrapping paper.

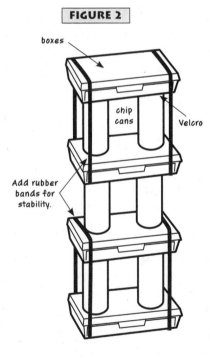

FIGURE 2

boxes

chip cans

Velcro

Add rubber bands for stability.

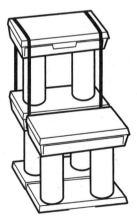

FIGURE 3

Box can be opened and flipped over to adjust shelf height.

SNEAKY CLEANERS YOU CAN MAKE

Some home cleaning products include toxic chemicals. You can substitute safer household ingredients that are easy to make and economical too.

Sneaky substitutes for polishing and general cleaning can be prepared very quickly by using common ingredients. Substituting even one of your conventional cleaners with a sneaky replacement will make a big difference.

WHAT'S NEEDED

- Vinegar
- Water
- Lemon juice
- Borax
- Olive oil
- Spray bottles

WHAT TO DO
All-Purpose Cleaner

To make an all-purpose cleaner: Mix 1 teaspoon of borax and ½ teaspoon of dishwashing liquid with 2 tablespoons of lemon juice in a 1-quart container of hot water. Then pour the solution into a spray bottle and spray on surfaces or on a towel, and simply wipe the surfaces until they are dirt free.

Glass Cleaner

For an easy-to-make glass cleaner, add a ¼ teaspoon of liquid dishwashing detergent to a ¼ cup of white vinegar. Then add 2 quarts of water and pour into a spray bottle. To use, simply spray the glass cleaner and wipe dry with an old newspaper.

Furniture Polish

There's no need to buy costly furniture polish when a sneaky substitute is on hand. Add 1 tablespoon of olive oil and 2 teaspoons of vinegar to 2 cups of water, and pour into a spray bottle. If desired, add ½ cup lemon juice for a pleasant fragrance. Mix the solution and you're ready to polish.

SOLAR COOKER PROJECT

One large piece of cardboard and aluminum foil is all you need to demonstrate the power of solar cooking. Reflective solar cookers generate no smoke or pollution making them safer than many other cookers. (Millions of children die each year from respiratory infections caused by cooking indoors with wood and other matter.)

WHAT'S NEEDED

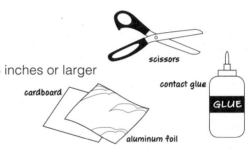

- Cardboard, 11 inches by 15 inches or larger
- Aluminum foil
- Contact glue
- Scissors

WHAT TO DO

This solar cooker project is designed from a single sheet of rectangular cardboard that stores flat. The dimensions are not critical, but it should be large enough to accommodate a small dish or pot when placed in the center area.

Cut a sheet of rectangular cardboard into the shape shown in **Figure 1**. Notice the diagonal slits on the bottom corners and the areas to be cut from the outer edges upward toward the center. Next, cut a piece of aluminum foil into the same size as the cardboard and glue them together. Then, carefully cut similar slits to match the cardboard version.

Next, fold the bottom section straight upward. Fold the upper side sections toward the bottom section and push the corners through the slits and bend them back to secure them in place. The solar cooker should look like the version shown in **Figure 2**.

Place your foodstuff in the solar cooker's center area and place it in the sun. Adjust the angle of the cooker to follow the sun's path as needed. Depending on environmental conditions, cooking with the solar cooker can take about three times longer than cooking an item in the traditional manner.

FIGURE 1

Cut cardboard into size and shape shown.

Cut slits and lines on cardboard.

Glue aluminum foil to cardboard and cut lines and slits.

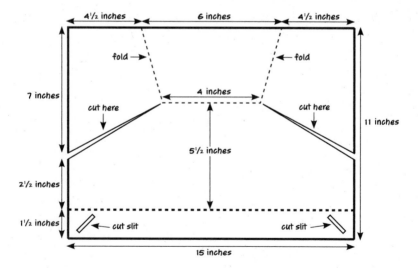

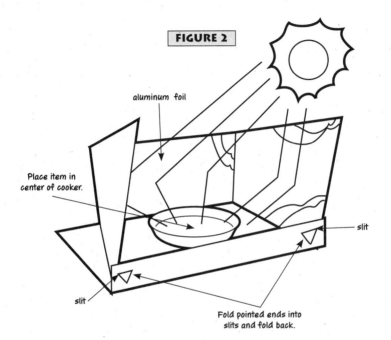

FIGURE 2

aluminum foil

Place item in
center of cooker.

slit

slit

Fold pointed ends into
slits and fold back.

SNEAKY SOLAR MOTOR

With just a few household items you can make a neat solar-powered motor, and it makes a great demonstration project for science class.

WHAT'S NEEDED

- Aluminum foil strips, 4 inches by 1 inch
- Tall, clear jar with lid
- Black marker
- Thread
- Tape

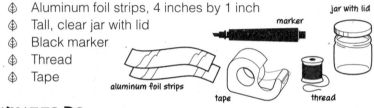

WHAT TO DO

First, cut two strips of aluminum foil into 4-inch by 1-inch strips and cut a slit in the center of each strip. Use the marker to darken the right third of both strips on both sides and fold the ends upward. See **Figure 1**.

Next, slide one strip into the other so they resemble a four-sided star wheel. The ends of each strip should point downward with all of the darkened ends in the same direction. Cut a 3-inch length of thread and carefully tape it to the center of one of the foil strips and to the underside of the jar lid, as shown in **Figure 2**.

Last, place the lid on the jar and position it in the sun. Soon, the foil blades will start to spin because of the difference in the heat absorption capabilities of the bright foil area compared to the darkened section. See **Figure 3**.

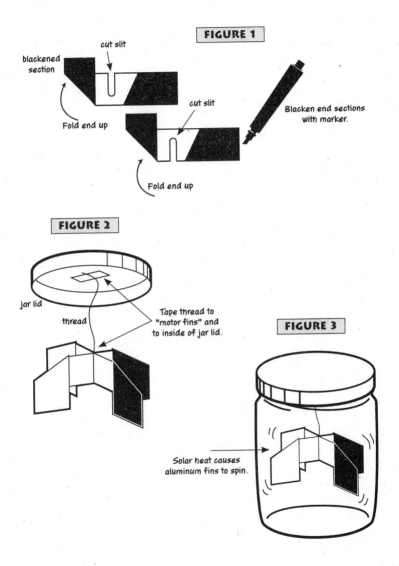

FIGURE 1

blackened section

cut slit

Fold end up

cut slit

Fold end up

Blacken end sections with marker.

FIGURE 2

jar lid

thread

Tape thread to "motor fins" and to inside of jar lid.

FIGURE 3

Solar heat causes aluminum fins to spin.

SNEAKY HOME AND VEHICLE ENERGY CONSERVATION TIPS

Home Energy Saving Tips

Try the following easy-to-implement energy conservation tips to reduce your energy bills.

- Repair leaky faucets, particularly a hot water faucet that can burden your water heater. You could waste up to 165 gallons of water per month from a single leak of one drop per second! Also, keep a cup of water in the refrigerator to prevent running water until it's cold—a running faucet wastes up to 5 gallons of water per minute.

- To cut your water usage up to 40 percent, install low-flow aerator attachments to faucets and showerheads.

   However, even with low-flow faucets, most people still leave the water running while shaving and rinsing—and most of it is wasted. For big families that live in large homes with multiple bathrooms, you'll realize long-term water savings by installing motion-sensing faucets in both bathroom and kitchen sinks.

- Wear more clothing indoors to save energy in the winter. Each degree you turn down your thermostat saves approximately 5 percent in heating costs. Programmable thermostats save even more as they can be set to lower the temperature at night. To improve efficiency, clean or replace your furnace filters regularly.

- Consider installing ceiling fans in the summer to provide cooling that may lessen the need to turn on an air conditioner.

- When possible, cook food in your microwave oven as it uses up to 75 percent less energy than range ovens.
- Before you leave for a vacation, turn off the circuit breaker to the hot water heater.
- On average, taking a shower will only use about half the energy that a hot bath does.
- Install compact florescent bulbs (CFL) everywhere you can. They typically look like a thin-swirled tube. However, traditional bulb designs are also made in the CFL format.
- A 13-watt CFL is equivalent to a 60-watt bulb and saves money. However, CFLs must not be thrown away like a standard bulb—they MUST be recycled. Home Depot and other hardware retailers offer CFL recycling programs. Check with your local outlets for further information.
- Only use plug-in room deodorizers when needed as they constantly consume energy.
- Purchase and use LED lights for the holidays. They last longer and use up to 90 percent less energy than traditional lights.
- Purchase items in bulk to save gas and cash.
- Shop for the ENERGY STAR label on home appliances and electronic products.
- The U.S. Post Office and some electronics stores offer electronics recycling programs. See your local outlet for further information.

PLASTIC RECYCLING

Most plastic jugs and bottles include a Plastic Identification Code (PIC). Look for a letter and number (e.g., A1, A2) inside a triangular recycling symbol on the side or bottom of the container. **Figures 1** and **2** show a typical PIC symbol embedded into a water jug and juice bottle.

Seven groups of plastic polymers are used for product packaging applications:

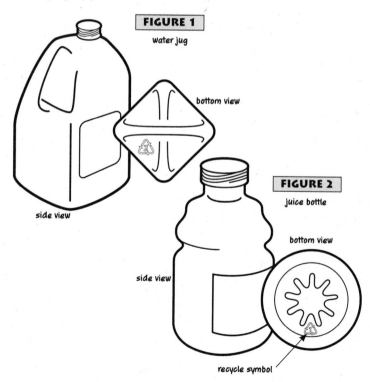

FIGURE 1

water jug

bottom view

side view

FIGURE 2

juice bottle

bottom view

side view

recycle symbol

A1 PET or PETE Polyethylene Terephthalate—Frequently used for soft drink and water bottles

A2 High-Density Polyethylene (HDPE)—Used for juice, milk, and water bottles and some retail bags

A3 Polyvinyl Chloride (PVC)—Found in plastic PVC piping and juice bottles

A4 Low-Density Polyethylene (LDPE)—Used for plastic cling wrap, squeezable bottles, and frozen food bags

A5 Polypropylene (PP)—Used for disposable cups and plates and reusable microwaveable ware

A6 Polystyrene (PS)—Used for disposable take-away containers, disposable cups and trays, and egg cartons

A7 Includes other plastic properties—Used in baby milk bottles and some beverage containers

Collect as many plastic discards as you can (don't forget to ask your friends, neighbors, and co-workers for theirs too) and bring them to your local plastic recycling drop-off centers. Note: Some recycling centers do not accept plastic with PIC codes higher than A2. Check with your local center for details about what items they will take.

PET OR PETE
(Polyethylene Terephthalate)
Recyclable

HDPE
(High-Density Polyethylene)
Recyclable

VINYL or PVC
(Polyvinyl chloride)
Not recyclable

LDPE
(Low-Density Polyethylene)
Recyclable

PP
(Polypropylene)
Recyclable

PS
(Polystyrene)
Recyclable

PC (Polycarbonate)
or PLA (Polyactide)
Not recyclable

BATTERIES, CHARGERS, AND POWER SUPPLIES

Only about one in six households recycles non-vehicle batteries. When possible, use rechargeable batteries and charge them with a portable solar recharger or a crank charger.

- ⊕ To maximize home electrical energy savings, install smart power strips that turn the power off when electronic equipment is not in use.
- ⊕ You can test your appliance power drain rate with a home electricity usage monitor.
- ⊕ Plug your lights into motion-sensing switch devices to automatically turn on and off when a room is not occupied.

GAS-SAVING TIPS

- ✦ Remove unnecessary items stored in your vehicle. Carrying around an extra one hundred pounds can reduce your mileage up to 2 percent.

- ✦ Use cruise control on the highway to sustain a constant speed and save fuel.

- ✦ Keep your vehicle's engine tuned and replace the air filters regularly.

- ✦ Keep your tires inflated according to manufacturer's recommendations. This can improve gas mileage up to 3 percent.

- ✦ Only use the manufacturer's recommended grade of motor oil.

- ✦ Save fuel and prevent wear and tear on your car by combining your short errands into one longer trip.

- ✦ If you own multiple vehicles, drive the one with the best gas mileage. And, if your job will allow it, try to telecommute.

- ✦ Consider using public transit if it is available and convenient for you. Join a carpool or a ride-share program. You can cut your weekly fuel costs in half and save wear on your car if you take turns driving with other commuters.

- ✦ Select a vehicle with a high fuel economy rating. The savings between a car that gets 20 miles per gallon and one that gets 30 miles per gallon driven approximately 12,000 miles per year is about $1,000 per year. See the Web site www.fueleconomy.gov to review the most fuel-efficient vehicles.

⊕ Aggressive driving (speeding, rapid acceleration, and braking) wastes gas. It can lower your gas mileage by 33 percent at highway speeds and by 5 percent around town. Vehicle gas mileage generally drops off at speeds above 60 miles per hour.

In fact, altering your driving habits can produce dramatic gains in fuel economy. An ultra passionate group, called the "hypermilers," go to amazing lengths to maximize their mileage gains. For example, they begin their journeys without starting their engines to coast as far as possible. Some hypermilers save gas by removing all excess items from their vehicles, including seats and spare tires!

For more information, see www.CleanMPG.com and www.greenhybrid.com.

ECO-
RESOURCES

Recommended Books

The following titles are in the same category as the Sneaky
Green Projects and Activities discussed in this book:

Consumer Guide to Home Energy Savings (American Council
for an Energy-Efficient Economy, 2003)

Sarah Callard and Diane Millis, *Green Living: A Practical Guide
to Eating, Gardening, Energy Saving and Housekeeping for
a Healthy Planet* (Carlton Books, 2002)

Jerri Farris, *10-Minute Energy-Saving Secrets: 250 Ways to Save
Big Bucks Year Round* (Fair Winds Press, 2006)

Joey Green,

——*Clean It! Fix It! Eat It!: Easy Ways to Solve Everyday
Problems with Brand-Name Products You've Already Got
Around the House* (Prentice Hall, 2001)

——*Clean Your Clothes with Cheez Wiz: And Hundreds of
Offbeat Uses for Dozens More Brand-Name Products*
(Renaissance Books, 2000)

——*Joey Green's Encyclopedia of Offbeat Uses for Brand-
Name Products* (Hyperion, 1998)

Vicky Lansky,

——*Another Use for 101 Common Household Items* (Book
Peddlers, 2004)

——*Don't Throw That Out: A Pennywise Parent's Guide* (Book
Peddlers, 1994)

Paul Scheckel, *The Home Energy Diet: How to Save Money by
Making Your House Energy-Smart* (New Society Publishers,
2005)

Society of Automotive Engineers, *Alternate Fuels: A Decade of
Success and Promise* (SAE International, 1994)

Crissy Trask, *It's Easy Being Green* (Gibbs Smith, 2006)

Vijay V. Vaitheeswaran, *Power to the People: How the Coming Energy Revolution Will Transform an Industry, Change Our Lives, and Maybe Even Save the Planet* (Farrar, Straus and Giroux, 2003)

Nick and Sheryl Wagoner, *Alternate Fuels: An Overview* (Thomson Delmar Learning, 2008)

Christine Woodside, *The Homeowner's Guide to Energy Independence* (Lyons Press, 2001)

MAGAZINES

Make
ReadyMade
Backpacker
Mother Earth News
E Magazine
Popular Science
Popular Mechanics

WEB SITES OF INTEREST

Recycle your shoes
    Giveshoes.org
    Letmeplay.com/reuseashoe
Reusablebags.com
Freecycle.org
Earth911.org
www.recycle.net
geektechnique.org
www.renewablechoice.com
www.sneakyuses.com
www.makezine.com
build-it-yourself.com

thefrugalshopper.com
frugalitynetwork.com
make-stuff.com
choose2reuse.org
ready-made.com
homepower.com
windpower.org
Smarthome.com
Doityourself.com
Mygreenelectronics.com
Epa.gov/bulbrecycling
Ewastedisposal.net
use-less-stuff.com
etoncorp.com